THE
RESURRECTION
GENERATION

L. Emerson Ferrell

Voice of The Light Ministries

THE RESURRECTION GENERATION

©Emerson Ferrell
1st Edition, 2021

COPYRIGHT

All Scripture quotations, unless indicated otherwise, have been taken from the New King James Version (NKJV) © 1982 by Thomas Nelson Inc., used by permission. All rights reserved.

Category: Reformation
Published by: Voice of The Light Ministries / U.S.A.
Cover Design: Ana Méndez Ferrell
Layout Design :   Andrea Jaramillo

Printed in The United States of America

www.voiceofthelight.com

Voice of The Light Ministries - P. O. Box 3418 Ponte Vedra Florida, 32004 / U.S.A.

ISBN: 978-1-944681-44-9

THE

RESURRECTION
GENERATION

L. Emerson Ferrell

CONTENT

THE
RESURRECTION
GENERATION

INTRODUCTION

There is nothing you will read in this book that you don't already know. That may sound like the worse possible way to introduce the reader to this book but keep reading. Just because you know doesn't mean you believe. You are reading this book because you know there is something greater and more wonderful that until now has been hard to find.

The Resurrection Generation describes those who have become what they know and as a result have been reborn outside this dimension controlled by the fear of death.

Regardless of your physical condition, religion, education, race, and beliefs, you are spiritually connected to God. That alone makes you the most powerful creature on this planet. But maybe you don't feel so powerful and in fact maybe you have never felt more afraid.

This book is written for you because if this book does anything, and it does, it will provide you with keys that until now have been hidden in plain sight. What does that mean?

Jesus said the kingdom of God was the single most important mission in our life and that it is impossible to find with your senses. We want to obey His word but how do we find what we can't see? I'm sure many of you have asked or are asking that question and many more will be, especially now during these extraordinary times.

This book will graphically demonstrate what is holding the real you from experiencing His kingdom now. You will learn that your origin and birthplace are dimensionally different, which has contributed to your not believing what you already know.

Moreover, you will stop immediately searching the physical dimension for your spiritual supply. Why? You will discover that nothing from this dimension can compare to the riches placed in you before the foundation of the world.

There is a term in quantum physics called "collapsing the wave function," which is used to describe energy becoming matter. It blows the minds of scientists because they cannot control or predict the outcome of events happening in that world.

Picture the waves emitted from throwing a rock into a body of water. The rock is The Holy Spirit, and His waves are love that when recognized will change your physical world. Everything physical originates from the love of God and it is why science and formulas are helpless to control or predict the spiritual dimensions of God.

The resurrection was the single most important event both visibly and invisibly because it opened the door to a realm even greater than the quantum, because Christ collapsed all dimensions into Himself.

This describes the place spoken about by Jesus when He said: nothing is impossible if you can believe. If you are willing to step into His spiritual dimension nothing is impossible. You will learn to experience the depths of that dimension each time you breathe in His mercy and exhale His grace.

Therefore, if you are resurrected in Him and you must know that you are, everything you need is already inside you. In other words, you are what you have been searching to find.

I told you this book will not tell you anything you didn't know, but because you didn't believe you created a world of lack, pain, suffering, doubt, and unbelief. The good news is Christ is calling you the way He did Lazarus out from your grave of unbelief and doubt to resurrect into the fullness of the first day light. The treasures of the universe do not compare to the knowledge of His resurrection.

The Church has been standing at the foot of the cross to long. The power of Christianity begins at the grave and never ends, which is eternity. You can discover God's glory and resurrection in the present. The eternal is in the present moment because it is timeless.

You knew this before the foundation of the world but now you must become what you know.

CHAPTER 1

SPIRITUAL
ENTANGLEMENT
IS THE SCIENCE OF LIFE

The most important revelation throughout this book is that we are spirit with a greater knowledge of the unknown than what we currently understand. However, unless you apply what you read nothing will change.

The first step to that realization begins through a conscious awareness of the present moment. Once we observe, the attention we surrender to the subconscious programs, playing like a lullaby in our mind, the faster we return to our origin. We arrived on this planet with the sin consciousness of Adam, which is unbelief and fear.

I am not writing this from a philosophical point of view but from extended journeys outside time and space in the presence of Christ. My experiences began when I observed my thoughts and reactions to my perception of the environment. This was strange at first because it challenged all my religious programming and preconceived ideas but over time a new light began to appear.

The light was on the inside of me and changed the way the world looked on the outside. I later learned from the Spirit it was *The Light* of the first day in Genesis. Moreover, the phrase, "All things are possible to those who can believe" began to play louder and louder inside that light.

This book is a glimpse into a small part of who we are In Christ before we were born into this world. Everything you could possibly need or want on this planet pales to the knowledge of your origin.

In other words, because of His resurrection we are what we have been searching for, but to understand that requires unlearning some things and observing the rest. Let's begin.

First, there is no doubt that we are physically created from the elements of this planet and physical dimension, but that is not your identity. The building blocks for all material are tiny bits of energy classified as atoms. These invisible cornerstones of the physical realm are more spirit than matter. Why? They are

99.99999% energy and less than 0.1% material or matter.

That's right science validates that we are more spirit than matter, but science uses the word *energy*.

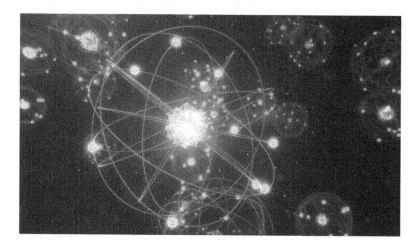

Fig. 1 - The Atom

Our spirit moves in and out of the invisible dimension around eight times a second. What does that mean? We are more wave than particle to use physics terminology, which means our source for life is spirit. Therefore, our spirit joins with the author of all life around 691,200 times a day. We are In Him as much or more than in the material dimension.

That knowledge alone should remove your fear of the physical world. The reason we aren't aware of that is because the majority of our attention is on the 0.1% matter, which keeps us unconscious of the present moment.

The eternal present moment is timeless, and it is the power that sustains our life. Until we are conscious of the present moment, we will never understand who we are and why God has placed you in this body.

Light is the common thread in all the dimensions because everything originated from the first day light, when God said: "Light be" (Genesis 1:3) Therefore, a deeper understanding of light is essential in our study and it is why we use physics to illustrate the spiritual parallel.

A. NEWTON AND REDUCTIONISM

Science and medicine are the offspring of the Greek philosopher Democritus who first coined the term atom, which means uncuttable. He taught that everything material is built from atoms and that the world is mechanical or a machine. Therefore, if a body is diseased it must be reduced to its smallest part to locate the problem.

Fig. 2 - Waves Becoming Particles or the Collapsed Wave Theory

The classical study of physics began by observing the physical earth and its laws of motion, especially gravity. One of the best-known physicists was Isaac Newton, whose observation of gravity and motion aided in his invention of calculus, to predict the movement of the planets. Once he knew the distance between objects, such as an apple falling from a tree, he could calculate the time it would take to hit the ground.

Therefore, classical physics introduced us to mathematics and computers to navigate confidently and accurately through the third dimension, or material world, where the speed of light is the common denominator. God created the physical realm inside the 4th dimension, which has been called time.

Think of classical physics as the science of the predictable. Mankind used mathematics to produce reliable and predictable equations that solved the problems of travel, electricity, communication, comfort, and economics to name a few.

Isaac Newton was a disciple of Democritus and is known for his classical laws of physics. His mathematical formulas provided the solution to build and repair physical objects, including man.

Newton was a theologian and undeniably a brilliant scientist, but he would always separate science and religion. When I use the word religion, I am referring to the organized system of worship that society considers acceptable.

Newton studied the Bible more than any other book but always separated the physical from the spiritual when discussing science, because the world system believes only what their senses can detect.

Science and medicine prescribe to the theory of reductionism, which is the belief that "the whole is the sum of its parts". Therefore, if one wants to understand or repair a machine it must be reduced to its smallest components.

Reductionism is the foundation for medicine because they view the body as a machine. Therefore, according to that belief the best way to repair a human body is to remove the organs believed to be diseased.

Students of science and medicine are taught to treat human beings as machines that function independently from God or Spirit. According to science the material world and nature are the most relevant factors in diagnosing disease. **In fact, the mission of modern science is to obtain knowledge in order to dominate nature.**

Everything in the physical dimension was both created and orchestrated by God before the foundation of the world. But science does not believe in what they cannot see or quantitively measure. Therefore, they discover what God created and proclaim the finding to be more relevant than the one who created it long before they were flesh and blood.

The world system promotes division because it allows for self-exaltation and notoriety, which is from the father of division, satan. Now, you can begin to understand why the world is so separated. This is what the fruit produced that man ate in the garden and what all branches of science promote.

As technology and equipment advanced, so did the desire to explore below the atomic structure. This subatomic realm puzzled science because it did not react or behave according to conventional laws that produced reliable results in the 3rd dimension. The startling observation in the subatomic dimension is still being investigated, producing more questions than answers.

Currently, Quantum Mechanics, offers the best language for bridging the visible with the invisible. The spiritual world is "unknowable" or understood from a mentality produced in this dimension and world system. Nevertheless, we are blessed to be alive at this time. Why? Because God is using this decade to stop the routines of people so they may discover whom they trust.

Religion uses the words good and bad or right and wrong. You may remember Adam's choice of fruit was from the tree of knowledge named "good and evil," or duality. The number 2 is the foundational digit for this world's system, because it represents duality. The wisdom of this world's system is confined to that knowledge and it is why people cannot comprehend the spiritual dimension without a new birth.

B. THE PHYSICS OF QUANTUM UNKNOWNS

Quantum Physics is defined as the study of the smallest units of light and energy. At the turn of the 20th century physicists such as Einstein, Planck, and Bohr built instruments using the technology of classical physics to study light. These brilliant scientists fully expected energy to behave like apples falling from a tree. In other words, they expected the same forces of gravity, motion, and mass to reproduce the same predictable results.

However, they soon discovered that the subatomic responded to their conscious observations. This is to say that when they looked for an electron or photon it would appear, but once they stopped looking it disappeared. I believe that discovery speaks volumes as it pertains to consciousness in this dimension.

Man's unconscious lifestyle is exactly why he believes life is random, but in reality, the kingdom of God is organizing a divine encounter for every human being on the planet. In other words, what man calls "chaos" is unpredictable to him but divine to God because what will arise is "manna for the wise" and "darkness to the dead".

Nevertheless, man is only capable of building and producing instrumentation from the mathematics of duality. For example, the operating system of computers is built upon 0 and 1, or duality. That limits mankind's scope as it pertains to understanding the dimensions of God's creations. Why? Because to know the mind of God you would need instruments from the spiritual dimension. The quantum realm reveals that man has no such instrumentation. This material will help you to divorce your faith and trust in science as your source for "truth."

The wisdom of this world is the result of cause and effect, right and wrong, good, and bad or duality. The foundation of man's world is the result of choosing to eat from the knowledge of good and evil.

Therefore, the wisdom of this world is incapable of discovering the ways of God. If Science possessed the keys to knowledge there would be no mysteries in the universe. You must understand this principle if you want to explore the spiritual dimensions.

There is a renowned experiment in Quantum Physics called "the double slit," which demonstrates that the subatomic level does not behave like the world of cause and effect. Physicists discovered that photons, which are small pieces of light, are unpredictable when they are not being observed.

Physicists such as Einstein and Plank soon discovered that energy is everywhere, all the time, until it is observed. Picture waves produced by a rock hitting the water. The waves are energy with a potential material outcome as long as it is being observed. Collapsing the wave is the description of energy becoming a particle.

Our thoughts interact with light, much like gravity does with mass in the classical model of physics. Science, in order to create mathematical formulas must be able to quantitively measure objects. However, unlike gravity, thoughts cannot be measured, thus the energy they produce changes it to matter, hence the term collapsing the wave.

In other words, the quantum realm is an ocean of potential outcomes that appear as a wave of energy that changes into particles or matter through the interaction with a subjective mind. The double slit experiment proved this phenomenon.

Double Slit Experiment

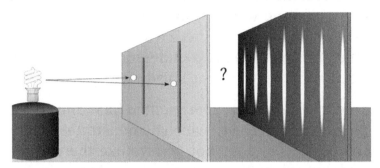

An interference wave pattern occurs without observation

Fig. 3

Double Slit Experiment

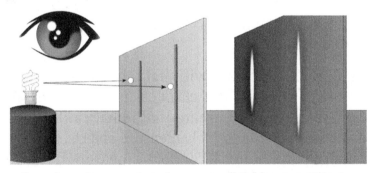

Conscious observance produces a predictable wave pattern

Fig. 4

The physical world of predictability operates according to the laws of gravity, light, mass, and motion. The subatomic dimension responds to laws man cannot understand or predict because that realm resembles the spiritual dimension of God. In other words, the quantum realm reacts to consciousness the same way God does to faith. What does this have to do with us?

In my opinion, we are waves of spirit, which is God's love, housed in a physical body with a mind. Is your mind "spirit" or "matter"? If you believe it to be the second, your senses will determine your reality. But if you have the mind of Christ the spiritual realm will be your reality.

Most typically we create our world according to our subconscious programming and subjective perceptions. How?

Our thoughts and beliefs interact with waves of potential changing the waves into matter. Faith is not the opposite of fear as many have been taught but rather a spiritual force that manifests whatever we believe either good or bad. We collapse the invisible waves of energy with our thoughts regardless of the matter it produces.

We are the thoughts of Christ before the origin of this world. This is why we must reconnect with His mind to understand our purpose and destiny.

Once we are reborn by the water and spirit our mind will be reunited with His mind. This is our origin and is reflected in this image.

Fig. 5 - Our Origin

The spiritual dimension responds to the hearts and minds of man. Jesus said it clearly:

> *That's why I tell you to have faith that you have already received whatever you pray for, and it will be yours.*

> **Mark 11:24**

Our study of the quantum realm reveals that science is validating what Jesus said thousands of years ago in Mark 11. God responds to faith, which requires a person seeing the outcome before it is manifested in the physical realm.

Nevertheless, I was taught to pray and wait for the physical manifestation of my request. This way of thinking is the result of believing we are incomplete and requires something from the outside to satisfy our needs. I now know that is not what Jesus taught.

My prayer life and the results changed dramatically after I learned to unite my heart and mind with my petition. We must rejoice immediately after asking God for something because that is faith. The power of faith is "seeing it" and rejoicing because you know your prayer is answered, and if we remain steadfast and don't doubt, the manifestation in the physical world will occur.

C. ENTANGLEMENT

Another concept that is important to understand is "The Entanglement Theory," which illustrates the authority of the spiritual dimension even in the material realm.

The term "quantum entanglement" is defined as energy from atoms, such as photons or electrons that remain connected even after being separated. Miraculously, whatever change is done to one affects the other one simultaneously.

For example, suppose you found a pair of dice that always equaled 9 regardless of how you tossed them. If you threw one dice and it revealed 6 you would know instantly the other dice would be a 3, because together they always equaled 9.

Suppose you flew a friend to the North Pole with one dice, while you kept the other in South America. Your dice was rolled and displayed a 5. Because of the entanglement theory you could determine the dice at the North Pole would be a 4.

Science is perplexed because nothing in our physical world moves faster than light. Everything on this planet and in our world operate according to the Newtonian model of physics, and Einstein's theory of relativity, which uses the speed of light as the constant. But how is it possible that entanglement works? Is there a speed faster than light?

Science calls that quantum or consciousness, but that is why they will never be the answer for the real problems on this planet, which is and will always be spiritual. I believe faith travels faster than light in all dimensions, including ours, which is the reason we experience miracles. This is spirit to spirit, and it is the communication between God and man.

We are equipped to know before we see it in the natural and that is what the Bible calls faith.

The Spirit will teach you to move at that speed once you devote your time to being conscious of his eternal present moment. **Eternity is in the now and it is the communication of knowing without learning**.

Mankind's fears demand science provides safety and security even if it is false. **Physics along with physicians create the illusion of safety and security but that requires our unconditional surrender to their authority. The result is our captivity to their pride and arrogance against the authority of God.**

Perhaps, the most profound result from the study of

entanglement is the reality that we are all connected through our spiritual Father.

> *Moreover, we have all had human fathers who disciplined us, and we respected them for it. How much more should we submit to the Father of spirits and live!*
>
> **Hebrews 12:9 NIV**

> *May the LORD, the God of the spirits of all flesh, appoint a man over the congregation*
>
> **Numbers 27:16 NIV**

The Father of "spirits" has joined us to Himself before the "foundation of the world." We are uncovering the depth of this truth.

Understanding our condition is the first step to change and it is one of the purposes of this book. The power of who we are is not found within the wisdom of this world. In fact, this world has no solutions and uses fear to hide their inadequacy.

The Light spoken by God on the first day is our origin. There is no separation in the world of energy and light, which is the building blocks for everything including the material dimension. That means we are one with God until we separate from Him by depending on the security and safety from this dimension. That is why science should never be the final word in any of your decisions at that respect.

Has the resurrected Christ taken control of your thoughts and desires or are you still trusting the science and governments of this world? That must be radically decided once and for all with no looking back as Lot's wife did.

We are spiritually connected to our Heavenly Father regardless of what your senses may be telling you.

Reality is where you are created not where you are born.

FIRST
DAY LIGHT

*Then God said, **"Let there be light"**; and there was light.*

*And God saw the light, that it was good; and God **divided the light from the darkness**. God called the light Day, and the darkness He called Night. So the evening and the morning were the first day.*

Genesis 1:3-5 NKJ

A. LIGHT AND SOUND ARE ONE IN HIM

You are determined to discover your origin because you know your beginning and end was finished before you were born into the world. The reason you know that is because you trust *The Word* that was made flesh and died for us. His resurrection made the way for all of mankind to return to their origin.

This knowledge has become more than a philosophy or religion for you and now is the time for you to stand in the reality of His victory over death. We are the generation of the resurrection, which means fear will leave the same way darkness did on the first day.

Our first step is the last step if eternity is our companion and not our destination.

In Genesis, God spoke LIGHT BE, which in essence is the only dimension that light and sound travel at the same speed. Think of that for a minute. Jesus wanted our eyes and ears to be open because they can see and hear Him without any time delay! **No separation! Knowing without learning!**

Have you ever heard a sonic boom? This occurs when an object such as a bullet or jet moves faster than sound. Living in Florida we often hear the sound of thunders, which is a sonic boom. This is the result of lightening exciting molecules that expands beyond the speed of sound.

The principles of sound and light are extremely significant to engineers building machines that function in the physical realm. In our 3-dimensional space we are limited by very finite laws governing the speeds of light and sound. That means when energy becomes matter its movement is restricted by time and space.

Therefore, as long as we depend on the material world for our resources and sustenance we will be restricted by these laws. The belief that we are matter is why fear dominates our thoughts. For this reason, it is very important to learn more and more about the realm of the spirit, which is our origin and nature.

> *For with You is the fountain of life; in Your light do we see light.*
>
> **Psalm 36:9 AMP**

The verse in Psalms is speaking about vision that does not require physical eyes. David is talking about the Light which both came from God and is Christ on the first day. That is the Light which is simultaneously visual and audible.

If we learn nothing else from this book it must be that our spirit is not restricted by the same laws that govern flesh and blood. Why? Because the real you is "in Him" before the creation of this dimension beyond your senses inside your spirit.

> *Every good gift and every perfect gift are from above, coming down from the Father of lights, with whom can be no variation, nor turning shadow.*
>
> **James 1:17 WEB**

The verse in James is describing The Resurrection Light, which is Christ. David and James are talking about the same light. James experienced it on the mount of transfiguration, which was the realm outside time and space. It is important to reread that event to understand just how mind bending it was.

He went on to say, "In solemn truth I tell you that some of those who are standing here will certainly not taste death till they have seen the Kingdom of God already come in power."

Six days later, Jesus took with Him Peter, James, and John, and brought them alone, apart from the rest, up a high mountain; and in their presence His appearance underwent a change.

His garments also became dazzling with brilliant whiteness—such whiteness as no bleaching on earth could give.

Moreover, there appeared to them Elijah accompanied by Moses; and the two were conversing with Jesus,

Mark 9:1-4 WEY

And He was transfigured before them, and His face shone like the sun, and His clothes became white as light.

Matthew 17:2 ESV

James is one of those witnessing a light so bright that not even bleach could describe the "whiteness" of His appearance. But the reality of what occurred on that mountain goes beyond all the laws that govern our world because they saw and recognized Moses and Elijah.

Imagine, visibly seeing, hearing, and recognizing two men who have been dead for centuries. How was this even possible? The light immersing Jesus removed all the laws governing the third dimension. Instantly, everyone was standing in eternity or transported to their origin before the foundation of the world. In other words, these men stepped outside the laws of time into the world of eternity that allowed them access to knowing without learning, which is God's kingdom.

In addition, Jesus said some will not taste death until they see His Kingdom and immediately, they were inside that invisible kingdom. This gives us an indication that death in this dimension is equivalent to the sense of taste.

In other words, seeing His kingdom numbs the taste of death, which is the opposite that happened to Adam when he tasted the fruit. Meditate on that for a minute. **The senses are the enemy of the spirit because they are not real. So how real is death?**

In addition, I believe they experienced *"The Light"* God released on the first day when He said, "Light Be." That light is more than illumination, it is the source for all life as well as God's Kingdom. Moreover, this is the light written about in Revelation chapters 21 and 22.

The journey back to our beginning is displayed in the following verses:

> *Jesus said, "It is I who am the light which is above them all. It is I who am The All. From me did The All come forth, and unto me did The All extend. Split a piece of wood, and I am there. Lift up the stone, and you will find me there."*
>
> **Thomas 77 (apocryphal)**

> *He is the image of the invisible God, the firstborn of all creation. For by Him all things were created in the heavens and on the earth, visible things and invisible things, whether thrones or dominions or principalities or powers. All things have been created through Him and for Him. He is before all things, and in Him all things are held together.*
>
> **Colossians 1:15-17**

> *In Him was Life, and the Life was the Light of men.*
>
> *There it was—the true Light [was then] coming into the world [the genuine, perfect, steadfast Light] that illumines every person.*

He came into the world, and though the world was made through Him, the world did not recognize Him.

John 1:4, 9-10 AMP

Christ, on the day He resurrected, removed everything that could hinder you and I from experiencing His Light and His Kingdom. The only thing that prevents our entering into that dimension is our unbelief. Nevertheless, when we are conscious of the eternal present moment, we both see and hear that light the same way, we move and breathe inside this world.

Christ stayed on the earth for 40 days after His resurrection, which is the same number of days God used to flood the first earth. The scriptures describe God's glory covering the earth, which in my opinion, was God's sign that He had restored the Garden back to the man. It's been here since His resurrection but hidden from those whose spiritual eyes and ears remain closed.

The Light functions in a completely different way than the natural light. The objects we see physically are displayed inside the occipital lobe. For example, that tree you see in broad daylight reappears inside your head in total darkness. Why is this important?

The light from this world is attached by frequency to emotions inside our brain. In other words, most of what we perceive is influenced by emotions, memories, and thoughts and just viewing a tree can create a flood of emotions that transport us from the present moment to an event in the past.

Light is more than illumination it is the frequency and source of everything visible and invisible. Thus, an encounter with the resurrected Christ exposes us to a frequency that illuminates not only scriptures but changes our perceptions of everything. Light exposes all the fears that hide inside the soul of man. The force of resurrection empowers love and destroys fear.

I believe you are reading this now because God wants you to experience a love beyond the emotions that until now have driven your thoughts and imaginations.

The verses below exposed my soul to a greater dimension of His love than ever before, and everything began to change from that point.

> *God's love for us has been manifested in that He has sent His only Son into the world so that we may have Life through Him.*
>
> **1 John 4:9 WEY**

> *"just as He chose us in Him before the foundation of the world, that we should be holy and without blame before Him in love,"*
>
> **Ephesians 1:4 NKJ**

These verses are landmark passages that pinpoint our location and origin. There are volumes that can be understood from these two passages, but arguably the most relevant, aside from beginning inside Christ, is that love is the foundation for everything both spiritual and physical.

Love arrives in the form of God's Son and satisfies all the requirements asked by The Father to redeem mankind. But that is just the beginning of what Christ did and is still doing, because love is the spiritual authority over everything visible or invisible.

The fact that you are reading this, demonstrates you have experienced the substance and reality from the light that does not produce shadows or darkness. Now you know the meaning of "in Him before the foundation of the world."

The authority over all things resides on the inside of all who trust the resurrected Christ. Do you believe that? If you do all that remains is for you to stay conscious of that truth.

By observing your thoughts, The Spirit will change your earthly perceptions. The things that frightened you will fade away like the snow on a sunny day. In addition, there will no longer be a past because the power of now removes time.

3

LIGHT IS
OR LIGHT WAS

We have just learned that spiritual illumination is not the same as physical light. We have discussed many times the frequency of light released by God in Genesis 1:3, which we refer to as 1st day light. Nevertheless, the importance of that light as it relates to our origin cannot be overstated.

We read earlier about the experience of the disciples with that light on the mount of transfiguration. All dimension, both visible and invisible were created from the Light of God on the first day.

Moreover, we are perpetually present with no future or past, which is why our spirit blinks in and out of the material realm 7or 8 times a second. In other words, we are eternal because we are In Him before there was a 4th day light to rule over the material dimension. This is so important for you to understand especially if you want to experience realty.

All light operates within the framework of frequency and information specific to the quality of light. What does that mean? The disciples witnessed a light that carried historical information that they instantly knew. That was 1st day Light.

The light our senses uses to process information is not the same light as the first day because it travels through the 4th and 3rd dimension, which means that nature of light physically enters time causing it to arrive thousands of years later.

For example, the light from the nearest star, Alpha-Centauri arrives in 4 years, while the light from the sun takes only 8 minutes but that is not exactly accurate and here is why.

Our sunlight originates in the Sun's core from tiny "packets of light" called photons. These are created by fusion inside the Sun's core, which begin as gamma radiation and are both emitted and absorbed countless times.

What you probably don't know, is that these photons were created tens of thousands of years ago and it took that long for them to be emitted by the sun. The sunlight we see is 170, 000 years and 8.5 minutes old. The light you use to illuminate your way was created millions of years ago. We don't see things the way they are, we see them the way they were.

Quantum physics discovered photons have no age and are timeless, which is the light of creation and our nature. The light of this world is historical, and both produces shadows and perpetuates the fear of death.

> *And this is the test by which men are judged—*
> *the Light has come into the world, and men*
> *loved the darkness more than they loved the*
> *Light, because their deeds were wicked.*
>
> **John 3:19 WEY**

In the beginning God separated darkness from light but never removed it. Therefore, Jesus was speaking spiritually when He described the worlds choice of darkness over Himself as The Light. Why? Because you will learn as you read that man lost God's image after he sinned. Mankind became the shadow of God the same way the law became a shadow of Jesus. Thus, man was comfortable living in darkness.

A. FREQUENCIES AND COLOR

An atom can have hundreds of electrons orbiting around its shell and as we know there are trillions of atoms that form material. Remember, atoms are pieces of energy that are more nothing than something.

Nevertheless, none of the trillions of electrons orbiting at eight billion times a second around the atoms ever collide. Therefore, what appears solid is actually waves generated from electrons passing so close to one another.

Fig. 6 - Waves from Non-Colliding Electrons

In other words, the floor you think to be solid are waves of energy closely packed together so that your physical body, which are electrons, can stand without passing through the surface.

These waves of energy create the illusion that objects are solid much like a spinning fan. The shorter the wavelength the higher the frequency, which is also relevant with our thoughts and color. When we feel love, we produce thoughts that appear ultraviolet in color and move at a higher frequency.

Colors that appear infrared in the light spectrum have a lower frequency and longer wave lengths. This is the signature that materials such as steel, iron, and plastics possess. Generally, thoughts that are sad, angry, depressed, and negative produce these types of wave lengths.

The fourth day light carries all color and frequencies as in rainbows, northern lights, and nature. Wavelengths determine the colors our eyes see, as in the rainbow.

Frequencies and wavelengths in our world determine the information our mind, brain, and bodies use to form thoughts and feelings. Moreover, our feelings and emotions produce waves and vibrations that are electromagnetic fields of energy.

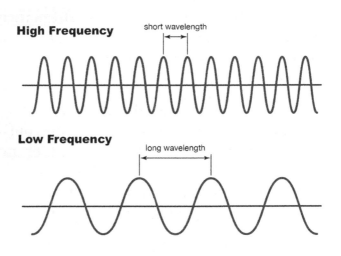

Fig. 7 – High and Low Frequencies

VISIBLE SPECTRUM

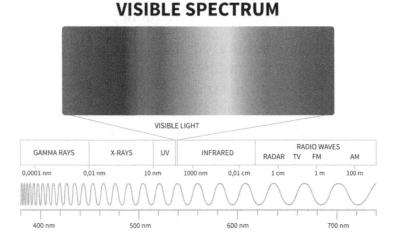

Fig. 8 – The Spectrum of Light

Before Adam fell there was no mention of colors because the Light of God or His Glory covered man, meaning he was brighter than the light created on the 4th day. However, after eating the fruit, his vibration or spiritual bandwidth decreased dramatically. In fact, had it not been for sin man would not have seen God's covenant with man called the rainbow. Interesting right?

Therefore, the result of his disobedience changed the frequency of light in this dimension, and our ability to see His glory in the earth. The further away we are, dimensionally, from the original source of light the denser we become and the harder it is for us to awaken to our original nature and purpose.

We live in the land of shadows created from unbelief, motion, gravity and preprogrammed beliefs that unconsciously influence our perceptions. We subconsciously respond to the images created by light in this dimension even if we know they are flawed by the influences of time, space, and shadows. For example, the light we see from the sun and stars is much different than the lamp beside our bed. Why is that important?

B. LIGHT AND BRAIN

The brain is a record of the past and responsible for the chemicals equal to the thoughts we have from our preconceived ideas and beliefs. For example, when you feel depressed the hypothalamus in your brain triggers a host of chemicals including cortisol, serotonin and dopamine that unites the body and mind with the emotion. Why is this important?

If you believe thoughts have something to do with your condition, then the way you feel will dictate the thoughts you think. Thus, because our bodies become addicted to the chemicals our thoughts produce, over time you will be unable to think greater than your feelings.

The speed of light from this dimension is the constant for mathematical formulas that science uses to build computers and technology that make our lives comfortable and predictable. Science has convinced the world that because of their technology and sophisticated computers they can protect mankind from the unknown.

But wait, have you stopped to consider the technology they use to convince mankind to trust their predictions are manufactured within the limitations of this dimension?

Scientists find what they are looking for, because they build equipment and instrumentation within the confines of this dimension. In other words, it is impossible to measure dimensions and realities outside their subjective reasoning because, as we learned our thoughts change the outcome in the quantum realm. **Remember, the quantum most resembles the spiritual dimension because it contains oceans of potentials that respond to faith.**

Therefore, in most cases the knowledge we value as scientific and reliable for our safety and security is subjective at best. The word subjective defines the reason why the subatomic realm is unpredictable to science.

Science, as we just said is neither acquainted with nor understand the characteristics of light from the first day. The light from this dimension is measurable and predictable and will not provide illumination to perceive the invisible.

Therefore, if we want to discover the ways of the Spirit and the realms of the invisible, we should become familiar with our spiritual nature and not rely on instrumentation from the third dimension.

My greatest realization after I experienced the resurrected Christ was that my senses were useless for discerning that truth. This is a good time to remind ourselves that **reality is discovered where we are created not where we are born.**

Nothing is static in this dimension. That means everything is moving or dynamic. The sooner you understand this, the faster you will stop trying to hold on to material things. Let go!!!

For example, our physical bodies are actually spinning atop the earth at 1000 miles an hour while it hurls around the sun at 18 miles a second. The solar system is traveling at 140 miles per second inside the milky way galaxy. Yet consciously we have no concept of that movement because of laws that govern this dimension.

All these forces change the frequency of light and our perceptions of objects in this dimension. Therefore, if we are unaware of the motion that we are experiencing every second, then, **perhaps we are also oblivious to the dramatic transformation that occurred at the resurrection of Christ.**

The 3rd dimension was created for man to dominate and regardless of the shadows and quality of light in this world the sons of resurrection reflect a different light. We are to reflect the glory of the resurrected Christ.

Amen

To use science terminology, time and space collapsed on themselves after Christ resurrected, thus changing the frequency and vibration we have access to within this dimension.

In other words, the kingdom of God is here, now, and accessible to all who are baptized into His water and Spirit. We see His kingdom when we stop looking at the material world as our reality. How do you do that?

Begin to celebrate the present moment and allow

the things of this world to harmlessly pass you by. If you practice staying present, He will shower you with His frequency of love and mercy.

Trust me, over time you will desire more the stillness than the noise. The result will be that you fight to stay present because you know the heavenly Father takes better care of you than He does the birds.

C. DIMENSIONAL DELIVERANCE OF PRIDE

You know that you are spirit, which means we are designed to understand dimensions beyond our senses. The following is very important to understand! Therefore, when we consciously practice His presence we will immediately begin to thank God for each incredible moment because we know there will be another one more precious than the one we experience right now.

Each second is a piece of eternity wrapped as a gift to you. Can you feel how extraordinary that gift is? We have no guarantee of another one. That is why each second must be celebrated with your attention. When you realize this as more precious than all the gold or silver on the planet your life has changed!

Fight to stay present while you study this section because it will deliver you from a false belief that we all have had to endure.

> God said, "Let there be lights in the expanse of the sky to divide the day from the night;

and let them be for signs to mark seasons, days, and year and let them be for lights in the expanse of the sky to give light on the earth;" and it was so.

God made the two great lights: the greater light to rule the day, and the lesser light to rule the night. He also made the stars God set them in the expanse of the sky to give light to the earth, and to rule over the day and over the night, and to divide the light from the darkness.

God saw that it was good. ***There was evening and there was morning, a fourth day.***

Genesis 1:14-19

Between the 1st and 4th Day there were infinite dimensions created from the combined frequencies of God's voice and His presence. It is important to understand that nothing God creates is linear. Everything He creates is multidimensional, orderly, and overseen with His love and grace.

Therefore, the expansion of the visible galaxies reflects His invisible dimensions. Moreover, His light and voice are the source and substance of light that both gives life and meaning to all things.

God formed man from the elements of this dimension, but his true nature as spirit had dominion over both visible and invisible. He was formed from the Word which is all things visible and invisible.

The sin of Adam had a ripple effect not only in the 3rd dimension but throughout all dimensions created from the first day light. The verse from Paul illustrates the spiritual hierarchy at creation.

> *For our struggle is not against flesh and blood, but against the rulers, against the powers, against the world rulers of this darkness, against the spiritual forces of evil in the heavens.*
>
> **Ephesians 6:12 NET**

Therefore, the powers and principalities and rulers corrupted by pride even in the invisible dimensions were exposed with Adam's sin. Pride, which was found in Lucifer, was the result of free choice and it is the spirit that will destroy all creation unless it is removed. Do not believe for one moment this caught God off guard. This was the perfect plan that only the Godhead knew before the foundation of the world.

The power of satan is the darkness of his light, which is the wisdom of this world system. Remember, he was God's light barer, so he understood the dimensions of light and how to twist the truth. Nevertheless, the most powerful proclamations made in hell by Christ was both visible and invisible within His resurrection light.

> *In it He also went to proclaim His victory to the spirits kept in prison.*
>
> **1 Peter 3:19 GW**

Resurrection destroyed darkness and the powers over it in all dimensions both visible and invisible. That act and proclamation returned everything to its origin. The result was and is, the invisible became visible to all who would enter God's Kingdom through the resurrected Christ.

Our attention to the physical material depletes our spiritual authority and eventually allows pride and fear to rule our life. The more our attention is on the present moment the more timeless we remain. In other words, we are operating equivalent to our origin.

We are eternal, which means death and fear are concepts of time, making them illusions. In fact, time only exists when you feel separate from what you perceive. The third and fourth dimensions are created as the result of man's separation from God.

Everything inside the dimensions of space and time, which means all material, is governed by fear. Our spiritual comprehension of who we are in Him before the foundation of the world gives us authority over matter.

We are no longer separate from eternity because of His resurrection making the laws of time and space irrelevant. Do you understand why Jesus said the only priority we have in this dimension is to find His kingdom?

D. THE SONS OF RESURRECTION

The fourth day light that influences the consciousness of this world was changed on the day Christ resurrected but our unconscious programming can only be changed with conscious observation.

Man was created to have dominion over the physical dimension, including death, but his desire for wisdom forced him to be a slave to his senses. All creatures unconscious of Christ are governed by the laws in this dimension.

The resurrection of Lazarus is one of the most fascinating accounts by John. I want to call your attention to why I believe Jesus waited until the fourth day to resurrect his friend Lazarus.

Take your Bible and turn to John 11 and study the words spoken by Jesus, something will happen to your spirit.

> *So Mary and Martha [the sisters] sent someone to tell Jesus, "Lord, the one you love is sick." When Jesus heard this, he said, "This sickness will not end in death. It is for the glory of God, to bring glory to the Son of God." Jesus loved Martha and her sister and Lazarus. But [or So] when he heard that Lazarus was sick, he stayed where he was for two more days.*

John 11:3-6 EXB

We know that Jesus was remarkably close to the family because of how often He stayed at their home.

One of the hardest things to do in ministry is to follow the instructions of The Spirit when those directions appear unloving.

Mary and Martha were sad and distraught that Jesus delayed His coming for their brother. Nevertheless, Jesus obeyed His Father and waited until the appointed time to go because He knew God would honor His obedience.

In the natural this would be very difficult to obey because of the love for this family. But one thing I have learned is that God's plans are not determined by the limited emotions from this dimension. He makes decisions that change generations forever and if we don't trust His wisdom, we will lean on the understanding from this world.

> *Jesus answered, "Are there not twelve hours in the day [of daylight]? If anyone walks in the daylight, he will not stumble, because he can see by* ***this world's light*** *[the sun]. But if anyone walks at night, he stumbles because* ***there is no light to help him see [the light is not in him]."***

John 11:9-10 EXB

Here is one of the most important issues of this chapter. Jesus is teaching the disciples about the difference between the light of this world and *The Light* in them, who is the source of all light.

The light of this world provides illumination for our senses and is limited to twelve hours. Our senses were crowned by Adam's choice as the god of this world. As a result, man uses that light to promote his pride and greed, which reproduces the same result generation after generation. Remember, Solomon said there is nothing new under that light.

We are formed from the original *Light* that defines us as sons of resurrection to reproduce the light of the first day without limits. We are going to say this in so many different ways so you will never be the same.

When Jesus arrived, He learned that Lazarus had already been dead and in the tomb for four days. [Some Jews believed that a soul would stay near a body for up to three days after death.]

Martha [then] said to Jesus, "Lord, if You had been here, my brother would not have died. But I know that even now God will give You anything You ask." Jesus said, "Your brother will rise and live again."

Martha answered, "I know that he will rise and live again in the resurrection on the last day." [Many Jews, particularly Pharisees, believed in a future bodily resurrection.]

Jesus said to her, "I am the resurrection and the life. Those who believe [The one who believes...] in Me will have life even if they die. And everyone who lives and believes in Me will never die. Do you believe this?"

Martha answered, "Yes, Lord. I believe that You are the Christ [Messiah], the Son of God, the One coming to [who was to come into] the world."

But Mary went to the place where Jesus was. When she saw Him, she fell at His feet and said, "Lord, if You had been here, my brother would not have died."

John 11:17,21-27,32 EXB

Jesus arrives at Bethany on the fourth day to find his beloved friends sad and depressed even though they had seen the miracles He had performed. Have you noticed how easy it is to believe and expect the worse possible outcome from circumstances?

For example, you arrive home from the most glorious visitation of God in your life only to find a foreclosure notice in the mail. Almost immediately your mind takes you to the worse possible scenario and outcome. Why is this?

The fear of death is subconsciously programmed into every child born into this world. Moreover, **the light from this dimension, as the result of sin, makes it extremely easy for unbelief and doubt to control our thoughts**. Even when we know better, we find it much easier to submit to the voices of lies rather than faith.

Martha and Mary both knew Jesus was the Messiah but were still troubled by the fear of death. In fact, in verse 39, Martha thought because Lazarus stunk God's resurrection power would be ineffective.

Then Jesus said to her, "Didn't I tell you that if you believed you would see the glory of God?" So they moved the stone away from the entrance. Then Jesus looked up [raised His eyes] and said, *"Father, I thank You that You heard Me. I know that You always hear Me, but I said these things because [for the benefit] of the people here around Me.* I want them to [so that they might] believe that You sent Me." After Jesus said this, He cried out in a loud voice, "Lazarus, come out [forth]!" The dead man came out, his hands and feet wrapped with pieces of cloth.

John 11:40-44 EXB

We are all born into the light of this world as Lazarus. When I say light, I am speaking of the wisdom and illumination inside this dimension. But we were in Him before the foundation of this world and not this world's illumination but until now many people did not know the difference.

Moreover, Jesus transformed the fourth day light into His consciousness of life and *light*. Jesus is calling you from the dark light of the cave where you lie in the grave clothes of doubt and unbelief. But if you listen closely you will hear "light be." Now, you are no longer slaves to the light of this world because you hear and see *The Light* of the first day.

All of us who are in Christ before the foundation of the world witnessed both the resurrection and the destruction of evil before we were born on this planet. Death and the fear of death cannot live in the timeless eternity of the first day *Light*.

> *For indeed they cannot die again; they are like angels and are sons of God through being* **sons of the Resurrection.**
>
> **Luke 20:36 WEY**

Notice that the verse says we are sons of God, which is the byproduct of resurrection. Jesus was born as the resurrected son of God before He endured the cross. Remember, we originate outside the mentality and laws of this dimension, which is linear.

Therefore, your origin is the prerequisite of your being a son of God, which means you are the son of God now! Nothing in the future will make you any greater than who you are from before the foundation of the world.

The light of this world produces the frequencies of fear inside the hearts and minds of the people. The power of *His Light* is the knowledge of resurrection. The resurrection generation are those that do not respond to the frequencies inside the light of this world.

We are the illumination for this dimension, the eternal *Light*, which has no past or future. Did you get that? We are the resurrected sons whose *light* is more brilliant than the light of this world.

Christ was raised on the third day and that is because He is both the kingdom and the completion of the

Law. Christ restored what Adam lost and destroyed the one who had the power over death, which is the devil.

The third day is the physical account of the prophetic fulfillment of all things both visible and invisible. You and I are both the physical and spiritual heirs of the third day glory of God. We are the reflection of the true glory and resurrection of Christ created to reflect that glory in this dimension as the eternal *light*.

We are *the light* that rules time and space in this dimension because we are the sons of resurrection. Live each day as that son, who is found in the timeless present moment.

CHAPTER

4

YOU ARE
B E F O R E
the world began

The scriptures that record the phrase "before the foundation of the world" highlight the discussion of this section and you will learn that "the world" is the consciousness of man without Christ.

Father, I desire that they also whom You have given Me be with Me where I am, that they *may see My glory, which You have given Me, for You loved Me **before the foundation of the world.***

John 17:24 WEB

*even as He chose us in Him **before the foundation of the world**, that we would be holy and without blemish before Him in love;*

Ephesians 1:4 WEB

*who was foreknown indeed **before the foundation of the world**, but was revealed at the end of times for your sake,*

1 Peter 1:20 WEB

The scripture uses the words *earth* and *world*, but as we will see they do not mean the same thing. The Greek words for world are *Cosmos* and *Aeon*, which means "ages" or "times".

Therefore, when the Bible speaks about the *world* it is not describing something physical but rather the collective thinking of the people on the earth.

Whereas *earth* is defined in the Hebrew dictionaries as "soil, ground, or dirt". In other words, according to the dictionaries earth is physical or matter.

Therefore, when you read John 3:16 it makes perfect sense that Jesus died for the sin consciousness of the planet, which originates in the soul of man.

Here is something that will help you. Think of the *earth* as your body and the *world* as your mind. This illustrates the power of thoughts in relation to our body.

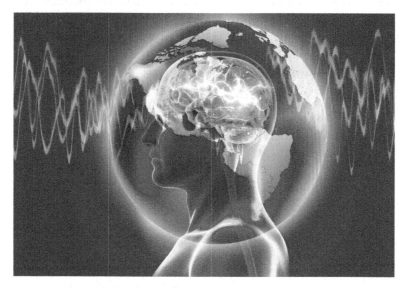

Fig. 9 - Man's Thoughts and Frequencies Create His World

God created all things both visible and invisible, nevertheless God's world is His invisible kingdom. Therefore, when Jesus spoke about His Kingdom, He was referring to God's invisible world.

In addition, He said the words that He speaks are spirit, which means He is communicating with the kingdom language of faith directly to your spirit. This is so important for you to understand. Communication is done spirit to spirt in God's kingdom.

Adam was created fully equipped for living simultaneously in both the visible and invisible realms. Therefore, the plan of God was for every generation of flesh to live spiritually connected to Him on the earth.

Adam's disobedience activated his senses and made him afraid. Since that event, all human beings are born afraid of death and programmed to believe the material world is their home and reality.

Jesus redeemed mankind because He was the Word before He was flesh. Therefore, His words below illustrate that His resurrection would deliver both the soul and body of mankind.

> *Now is the judgment of this **world**: now shall the prince of this **world** be cast out.*
>
> *And I, if I be lifted up from the **earth**, will draw all men unto myself.*

John 12:31-32 NSV

The passages illustrate that Jesus judged both satan and his kingdom at resurrection. The authority given to satan by Adam was removed through the resurrection of Christ. Do you see that? The authority Christ returned to us depends on our ability to live in His kingdom now.

The importance of those verses cannot be overstated. Jesus was born the son of man with the consciousness of His Father. His assignment was far greater than physical death but if people only see Jesus of Nazareth on the cross, they will not see Him as the Christ.

An important step that helped me understand this transition was to observe the way He exchanged His will for His Father's. He trained Himself as ⁚ be conscious of the moment.

In other words, He disciplined His spirit to pay attention to everything His Heavenly Father did and said. That means He did not have an opinion or exercise His will.

Moreover, He did not assume the persona of Jesus of Nazareth; He was the son of man. This was because He spent hours alone with His Father. Jesus was consumed with His Father and that is why He resurrected.

We become what we consume, which is why I recommend fasting. If we want His reflection stop consuming the images from this world.

Most people assume a personality from imagining and thinking about anything but the now. Their persona becomes their identity, which consumes their time and thoughts. They become what they consume, which is material and not spirit.

I challenge you to spend time observing your thoughts. Most people are uncomfortable being still or silent because of hidden fears of some sort or another. Until you conquer that fear peace and stillness will be your enemy.

Our thoughts, both create and define the world we experience.

The two important questions we must answer is who are we and where are we from? Are you the son of resurrection or are you a personality from this world?

Your faith is ultimately in the world you identify as your origin. If this planet is your home, you will be forced to function by its wisdom and your senses. However, if you determine that you are In Him before the foundation of the world you must learn the language of the spirit, which is faith.

We have discovered the importance of our thoughts in relation to our world. If we remain In Him as the scriptures depict, our thoughts will be different than if we identify as citizens of earth. Why? Because thoughts have a frequency and vibration that attract heaven or hell.

 Living in His kingdom depends on a continual encounter with the living Christ, which means the authority of resurrection rules over the fear of death. Each day must be a new and fresh experience with that relationship, or you will build a religion from yesterday's experiences.

After Jesus resurrected, His disciples did not recognize Him, even the ones that saw Him in this state more than once. Why? Because the dimension of eternity is neither familiar or predictable, otherwise it would exist in time and be governed by fear.

If we are In Him, and we are, our thoughts and experiences will not be the same. Those who know they are spirit renew their spirit by focusing less on matter and more on spirit. In other words, stop thinking about the past or future and observe the present.

A. THE WORLD AND SIN CONSCIOUSNESS

We now know that *world* and *consciousness* are words that help our soul understand its relationship with eternity. We must believe and know that the resurrection of Christ destroyed the consciousness of fear and death, which is the foundation of this world. That knowledge awakens our spirit to God's Spirit, which returns heaven to our life.

This verse from the letter to the Ephesians is written outside this dimension and inspired me to search the depths of what Paul witnessed.

> *Even before the world was made, God had already chosen us to be His, through our union with Christ, so that we would be holy and without fault before Him. Because of His love.*
>
> **Ephesians 1:4 TEV.**

The reality of that verse will perpetually unfold inside everyone who pursues the love of Christ and the limitlessness of His resurrection.

The most powerful word in Christianity is resurrection because it proves Jesus was not a philosopher or a religious martyr but indeed the source of all life. He is the fulfillment of every prophesy written about Him in the Bible, especially in Genesis 3:15.

> *I will make you and the woman hate each other; her offspring and yours will always be enemies. **Her offspring will crush your head**, and you will bite her offspring's heel.*
>
> **Genesis 3:15 NKJ**

God uses the same gender that was seduced by satan to produce the offspring that crushed the head of the liar. That is majestic on many levels but none so sweet as the way God redeemed the woman through the birth of His Son. His love and authority are visible for anyone desiring redemption.

The sin consciousness of this world began and will never change, because of the laws that were set into motion by disobedience.

God is righteous and will never change your right to choose, but that also means He is faithful to fulfill the consequences of those choices. Nevertheless, His love always makes a way for those who chose Him even after making wrong choices.

> *Of course, we may eat fruit from the trees in the garden, the woman replied. It's only the fruit from the tree in the middle of the garden that we are not allowed to eat. God said, you must not **eat it or even touch it; if you do, you will die.***
>
> **Genesis 3:2-3 NLT**

> **You won't die!** *the serpent replied to the woman. God knows that your eyes will be opened as soon as you eat it, and you will be like God, knowing both good and evil.*
>
> *He replied, I heard you walking in the garden, so I hid. **I was afraid** because I was naked.*
>
> **Genesis 3:4-5,10 NLT**

These verses are the foundation of "the world" and here is why.

Adam's body was clothed in the material of the earth, but that was not who he was and that is not who you are either. God provides us with the material necessary for our rulership and authority.

Mankind was created to rule over the earth, which means nothing from this planet can destroy man, including disease. If you do not get anything else from this chapter let it be that **our design is to rule and dominate both visible and invisible things on this planet.** That means nothing including germs and viruses are greater than His Word.

The conversation between the woman and satan is extremely important to understand. The woman attempted to make God sound like a tyrant by saying that He would "kill" anyone who would even touch the fruit, let alone eat it.

The woman saw the fruit as something that would make her wise. God created all mankind in wholeness and oneness after Himself. She used her senses to desire wisdom which was something she "believed was lacking." That desire separated her from wholeness. We are always separated from the things we desire until we realize we were created totally complete, lacking nothing.

Each time we experience desires and make choices from the outer world we are submitting to an unconscious program that demands separation because it was formed after the father of lies. Desires and fear originate in time, which separate us from oneness, because choosing what you already have makes you flesh not spirit. We are created whole with everything we need even if it is not visible.

The act of celebrating our wholeness through gratitude and thanksgiving removes separation and lack, because we express what we can't know in the material realm. In other words, by using faith, which in this example is thanking God for what is not visible, we change our perception from lack to wholeness.

The earth was formed to submit to the authority of God. **God gave man His authority by forming us in His likeness and image**. That power was on display in Adam when he named the animals.

Adam gave the creatures image and likeness the same way God imparted it to him. That means the creatures manifested the character of the name given them by Adam.

Adam had complete authority to change the nature and character of all living things in the material dimension including the solar system by joining his mind and heart in one accord. That is critical to understand.

Wholeness demands that we act in unity with both our mind and heart, which is the way man was created in the beginning.

Therefore, the earth and the world responded to the woman's decree of death and Adams's admission of fear in the same manner as the animals did to their names. In other words, the same laws that governed the planet physically were set into motion spiritually by sin. The verse below indicates the physical laws that govern this world and planet.

While the earth remains, seedtime and harvest, and cold and heat, and summer and winter, and day and night shall not cease.

Genesis 8:22 NKJV

Adam and his help mate, the gods of this planet, established fear and death as the spiritual substance for this world. Moreover, the foundation of this dimension is fear and death, which is the wisdom of this world.

Man is physically constructed from the material of the third dimension, which functions perpetually in duality or good and evil.

Therefore, sin consciousness is the spiritual virus that infects anyone who desires the wisdom from this dimension and ultimately eats of the tree of knowledge. The results are documented throughout history in wars, death, famine, sickness, disease, and chaos.

The verse below explains why God had to kill the virus before it wiped out all His creation.

*And the LORD saw that the wickedness of man was great in the earth, and that **every imagination of the thoughts** of his heart was only **evil continually**. And it repented* *the LORD that He had made man on the earth, and it grieved Him at His heart.*

Genesis 6:5-6 ERV

But Noah found grace and received the blueprint for the ark that would keep he and his family alive until the flood receded. Nevertheless, the sin consciousness remained in the earth and third dimension.

God restricted the physical movements of man by surrounding this dimension in time, some call the fourth dimension. Therefore, time and space along with the light from the fourth day are the governing factors in our world system.

Do you see the genius of God in creating the lights that rule over the physical earth on the fourth day while establishing a fourth dimension that rules over the souls of man inside the third dimension?

Spirits are not restricted by time and space, which means we have access to all dimensions In Him. Therefore, if what the scriptures say about our origin "in Him" before the foundation of the world is true, then we can experience the "New Birth."

The reality of what Jesus tells Nicodemus in John 3 means we have access to all dimensions outside time and space. Once we are reborn, the ability to remain In Him becomes our passion and first love. We will learn that His resurrection returned us to the garden because before there was time, we were In Him.

There are many writings not found in the canon of the Bible and the Gospel of Thomas is one such book.

Some of these books known as the "apocryphal" are a blessing to understand. They are parallel with the Scriptures and provide light in many cases and Thomas is one of those books. Jesus made a special effort to find him after His resurrection to demonstrate the power of resurrection.

> *Jesus said, "Whoever has come to understand the world has found (only) a corpse, and whoever has found a corpse is superior to the world.*

Thomas 56 (Apocryphal)

Jesus is clearly speaking about the sin consciousness that kills those who do not recognize that this world is the anti-Christ spirit. Those who refuse to eat of the fruit from this world system will soon understand their original status as Priests and Kings.

> *Jesus said, "I took My place in the midst of the world, and I appeared to them in flesh. I found all of them intoxicated; I found none of them thirsty. And My soul became afflicted for the sons of men, because they are blind in their hearts and do not have sight; for empty they came into the world, and empty too they seek to leave the world. But for the moment they are intoxicated. When they shake off their wine, then they will repent."*

Thomas 28 (Apocryphal)

In this passage Jesus is describing the condition of man at birth. The drunkenness is another way of saying we are hypnotized to believe we are flesh and helpless. If we remain conscious the drunkenness will pass and we will experience the resurrection of Christ, which will alter the way we think and believe.

> *Jesus said, "If two make peace with each other in this one house, they will say to the mountain, 'Move Away,' and it will move away."*
>
> **Thomas 48 (Apocryphal)**

> *Jesus said, "When you make the two one, you will become the sons of man, and when you say, 'Mountain, move away,' it will move away."*
>
> **Thomas 106 (Apocryphal)**

Jesus is illustrating that God created man to control the outer world from the inside. We learned earlier that fear creates separation in our soul dividing the heart and mind, but if we become one in our belief, it will transform matter. If we desire to make the two one, we must first consciously unite the division inside ourselves and then give thanks outwardly for the miracle.

The power of prayer is seeing the finished result in your mind before you pray and thanking Him from your heart regardless of the way it may appear.

The external world is the result of your belief. Change what you believe and what you perceive will change proportionately.

B. CHRIST IS CONSCIOUS INSIDE YOU NOW

The earth was restored through the resurrection of Christ, but not mankind's sin consciousness and subconscious programming. Physical death still occurs in this dimension because that is one of the laws governing the third dimension. We are repeating the verse in Genesis 8:22 to remind you of the laws set in motion by sin.

> *While the earth remains, seed time and harvest, and cold and heat, and summer and winter, and day and night will not cease.*

Genesis 8:22 NKJ

We are created to experience dimensions outside the restrictions of time and space. The challenge is that our subconscious program overrides our spiritual hunger and thirst to return and pursue what is physically undiscernible.

First and foremost, we must understand that knowledge from this dimension will not change our spiritual condition. Why?

Fear is the spiritual substance that creates the wisdom from this world and is the hardware and software that controls our subconscious programming. That software is inside all material but there is a back door[1] that God uses to change our lives.

My early Christian training and beliefs were the result of doctrines from both the Baptist and Pentecostal denominations. The average Christian is taught that God wants them to enjoy the abundant life until they die. The problem is that God's definition of abundance and ours are not the same. Ours produces more attachment to the material realm, which generally means make money, vote conservative, trust the doctor, and compete for success. All these things seem correct and wholesome, but it has nothing to do with God's idea of abundance or our design and destiny.

Spiritual abundance is having more than you need when you need it. Think of the manna that fell in the desert. God provided all they needed for each day, but the mentality of sin is not satisfied with today because fear demands worrying about the future.

The power of the cross and salvation through Jesus is the central messages from the pulpits of most Christian churches. Their belief of the gospel was and is the salvation message of Jesus Christ. The truth of what Jesus did for all of mankind is irrefutable, but it is only part of the glorious gospel.

Unfortunately, that powerful message was and is clothed in fear by the indoctrination of a future worldwide tribulation that requires Jesus to return and finish His work. I remember being unpopular

---

1 A backdoor in software or a computer system is generally an undocumented portal that allows an administrator to enter the system to troubleshoot or do upkeep. But it also refers to a secret portal that hackers and intelligence agencies use to gain illicit access

after telling people that I didn't believe that was part of the gospel. Why? Because, in my opinion the gospel should not produce fear but rather faith in His resurrection.

The Gospel is not a future event that requires a physical event to change our spiritual condition. **There was only one physical event that happened on this planet, which changed your life forever and that was the resurrection of Christ.**

C. SPIRITUAL DEATH DESTROYED

As I stated in the first chapter of this book, there is a term used in physics called "collapsed wave function" that describes a wave of energy becoming matter. However, in the world of science, death is another way of describing matter returning to energy.

If there is one word that strikes fear into the hearts and minds of every human being on the planet it is death. Physically dying is the natural outcome from a physical birth in this world, but unfortunately those who have not experienced His resurrection think about death more than life.

The invisible or spiritual dimension is the source for the material world including birth and death. Both physical and spiritual death, were destroyed by His resurrection, which means all things are new.

According to the first law of thermodynamics, energy cannot be destroyed or created. However, when Jesus speaks about death in Revelation it is called the second death, which seems to violate all the laws of this dimension. What does that mean?

> *Then death and Hades were thrown into the lake of fire.* ***This is the second death, the lake of fire.***
> **Revelation 20:14 NASB**

Jesus is speaking as the resurrected Christ that redeemed mankind from the laws sin produced, which was spiritual death, called "the second death". The laws that govern the third- and fourth-dimension function within God's plan, which is to draw all men back to Him through His unconditional love.

In other words, the fear of physical death ultimately produces a desire in people to consider eternity and their origin before the foundation of the world. God's love transcends time, space, and physical death but His love waits until man calls for His mercy and grace.

The Word became matter, as Jesus of Nazareth, to destroy death and fulfill the law. All physical matter ceases to live in that state but is that really death for you and me?

Are you flesh or are you spirit? Our body responds to our thoughts, which must be controlled by our spirit, if they are not, we will think about physical death and not resurrection life.

In most cases the unconscious program operating when we are not paying attention to the present moment, produces thoughts equal to death and dying physically. What is it to the real you that your body returns to the earth? Answer this question.

Before the crucifixion, death was the final authority in a person's life because of the sin of Adam, but His resurrection collapsed all dimensions into Himself, which is the beautiful picture of reconciliation.

> *And God purposed through Him to reconcile the universe to Himself, making peace through His blood, which was shed upon the Cross--to reconcile to Himself through Him, I say, things on earth and things in Heaven.*

Colossians 1:20 WEY

His resurrection destroyed death and annulled the events in Genesis that restricted mankind from his origin. Moreover, it opened the 5th dimension portal for man to sit with Him in the heavenly places.

Fig. 10 - Christ the Door to the 5th Dimension

Experiencing His resurrection and ever ascending nature opens the fifth dimension to the reality of our origin. His resurrection is an ongoing process we can enjoy inside the eternal present moment. If we want to experience eternity now, we must stay connected to the present. The sentences you just read are not a mental concept but rather a door home.

Nevertheless, the past and future will continually send images and sensations in the form of feelings to remove you from your position as eternal. The following scriptures are examples of those types of messages.

> *"So, don't worry about these things, saying, 'What will we eat? What will we drink? What will we wear?' These things dominate the thoughts of unbelievers, but your heavenly Father already knows all your needs.*
>
> *Seek the Kingdom of God above all else, and live righteously, and He will give you everything you need.*
>
> *So, don't worry about tomorrow, for tomorrow will bring its own worries. Today's trouble is enough for today".*

Matthew 6:31-34 NLT

Those frightened by death trust the systems of this world and have not experienced the resurrected Christ. The result is we clothe ourselves in the garments of pride and arrogance to hide from the one who loves you unconditionally.

That is exactly what happened to God's first man. They were frightened and afraid, so they hid. If we trust the wisdom of this world, it is because we ate the fruit of duality. If that is your condition, then now is the time to change what you believe. Nothing changes until you do.

Those of us In Him before the foundation of the world know our origin as spirits and are awakening to the Truth. The present moment, which is eternal, is the perpetual consciousness of Christ. Transformation occurs when we feel and think from the oneness of His Spirit.

WHAT IS THE
IMAGE of GOD

This is perhaps one of the most important parts of this book because everything in the physical dimension is both an image and reflection of the artist, which is our Heavenly Father. In fact, the physical realm in all its splendor was designed to be the pure reflection of His image. The way we perceive the physical realm says more about us than anything else.

> *And God saith,* **Let Us make man in Our image, according to Our likeness**, *and let*

> *them rule over fish of the sea, and over fowl of the heavens, and over cattle, and over all the earth, and over every creeping thing that is creeping on the earth.*
>
> *And **God prepared the man in His image; in the image of God, He prepared him**, a male and a female He prepared them.*
>
> **Genesis 1:26-27 YLT**

Notice in verse 27 the writer implies man was created inside a dimension in which only He lives. In other words, God The Father created man from within Himself, which is the dimension of all dimensions and the source of *The Light* without shadows. Returning to our origin not only changes our dimension but it also removes any limits from our thinking and believing. This is critical for you to understand.

I believe there were two reasons Moses was unable to describe in Genesis the dimension God was portraying.

Adam was formed from *The Light* without images. He was to be the physical image of the imageless God and reproduce generations on the earth after his image. In other words, Adam was endowed with all the characteristics to reproduce *sons of light* throughout the material dimension.

However, his sin formed an object between God and man that produced shadows. Adam's sin removed the image and likeness of God and made man a shadow of the image. Do you understand? Read this verse in Matthew and study carefully the words of Jesus as they pertain to light and darkness.

The eye is the lamp of the body. So, if your eye is unclouded, your whole body will be full of light.

But if your eye is evil, your whole body will be full of darkness. If the light in you is darkness, how dark it will be!

Matthew 6:22-23 GWT

Jesus is using the eye and light to recreate the scene in the garden of Eden. The woman saw that the fruit was pleasant and would provide wisdom. (paraphrasing)

The eye is the soul, and the light represents wisdom, which is still the case today. The soul chooses rather to believe the light or wisdom from this world or rediscover the *light* inside their spirit. Jesus defines the light of this world as darkness but to a soul separated from its source it appears as illumination.

As long as Adam remained in the image of God his soul would enjoy the purity and wisdom of God's *light*. However, once they ate from the tree of knowledge, darkness filled their souls.

God's first created man, who was made after His image and likeness could no longer reflect God's imageless *light* because an object called sin was between Him and man. Man is a shadow of the image and likeness of God because his soul became his wisdom and reality.

Maybe this analogy illustrates the object of sin between *The Light*, and Adam. A solar eclipse describes the passing of the moon between the sun and earth. The moon cast a shadow over mankind eternally, which is sin for the sake of this comparison. The soul of man is perpetually in darkness until *The Light* of the First day becomes his source.

The result is mankind has the image of Adam who bares the shadow of his creator but not His image. This illustrates why all creation is born with the sin consciousness of Adam on the earth.

Secondly, the reason we are challenged and limited in this dimension is because our thoughts are restricted by the light from our soul. In other words, all our perceptions are formed within the shadows of the soul. If you meditate on this, it will help you to remain conscious of your actions and behaviors.

God's mind has no restriction because He is the source of all life. Everything He creates is one of a kind and that means you. In other words, it is impossible for men to have a thought from their origin because their minds are born inside the sin consciousness of Adam.

All of our imaginations are the result of a picture of something from the external world. In other words, our minds are incapable of creating something that has never existed. But you may say what about the industrial revolution and modern-day inventions like cell phones or computers?

Shadows cannot create because they are not the source. Therefore, they assemble things from an imagination that originated in darkness and will never sustain life. Creations that form this dimension are in reality shadows creating more shadows with no substance. Nothing is new under the sun because we are living as the shadow of our Creator.

The central theme of our discussion is that all human beings are born within a limited range of possibilities as long as this system is their source for wisdom and reality.

The real you is formed from "Light Be," which means nothing from this dimension will satisfy or nourish your spiritual nature.

The Godhead formed man from their Spirit in love and perfection to reflect their divine imagination and purpose. We must become our true origin as The Light, which is the description of God.

Moreover, His *Light* is both imageless and without shadow, which means the **substance itself is the form**. Think about that for a minute.

In the material dimension we create a glass from material to hold a substance such as water. However, in the dimension of God, *Light* is both the substance and the image.

It is impossible to imagine God. The best we can do is to look for scriptures that describe His characteristics and substance. God is described in 1 John 4 as "love" and Jesus says in John 4:24, He is "Spirit". Paul says in Colossians 1:15 that He is "invisible", and Hebrews 11:3,6 says faith pleases God and through it we know that the visible world was created from the invisible.

Thus, God is love, invisible, Spirit and accessible by faith. All of these descriptions are ethereal or spiritual because they describe a being that cannot be conceived or understood inside this dimension. Moreover, His words are also from that dimension, which makes the verse in John 6:63 so important.

> *Life is spiritual. Your physical existence doesn't contribute to that life. The words that I have spoken to you are spiritual. They are life.*

John 6:63 (Names of God translation)

Our relationship with images is a key to understanding many things, but it is especially important as it relates to our trust in the material dimension. In other words, each time we connect an image with a memory or thought we have established a relationship in this dimension. Therefore, our attachment to the physical realm is why we believe we are flesh.

Our original nature is to recreate heaven on earth but in order for that to happen we must see His substance as the external world. How? That occurs when you realize what you see in the natural is a reflection of you. In other words, we are not separate from what we see when we are conscious of our origin *In Him*.

What we believe is released into the images we create. That means if you believe in sickness, disease, and death, the material from this dimension will cooperate with that belief. Moreover, the more our thoughts are consumed by those images the faster our reality reflects those thoughts.

God created all things from His imagination and gave man the same power. However, **we form our** state of being from what we think and feel, which creates our image not God's. Only God can create externally because there is no darkness inside Him.

> Abraham believed when he stood in the presence of the God who gives life to dead people and **calls into existence things that don't even exist**.
>
> **Romans 4:17 GWT**

He formed us within His *Light* and dimension to demonstrate our spirits are one with His. This requires your study to see the depths of who is inside you. Our physical bodies house God, which has no external image. Nevertheless, the one with no image formed the image of man. Think about that.

God created everything both visible and invisible from an everlasting well of possibilities. Our limitations are the result of our faith and trust in the material dimension as our source. In other words, **we don't see things the way they are, we see things the way we are.** A soul of darkness reproduces the same.

We are born inheriting the fears and anxieties passed down generation after generation from our families and cultures. Our subconscious programing creates our world through our imagination which is filtered by the light of the fourth day.

Unfortunately, most people are oblivious to that and believe the images they see of people, objects, and circumstances to be real. This determines the foundation we use to build our desires and dreams, as well as validate our images.

For example, if you believe governments and physicians are established by God for your wellbeing you will form positive images of their importance for your security and safety. This is why most people chose the advice of physicians over the word of Christ.

The sin consciousness inside the souls of man is constructed from the fear of death, which means the substance of everything we want from this world is fashioned from what we fear. **Moreover, the images we fear are the ones we serve**, because the foundations of this world control the masses with the fear of death.

> *Seeing, then, the children have partaken of flesh and blood, He Himself also in like manner did take part of the same,* **that through death He might destroy him having the power of death -- that is, the devil -- and might deliver those, whoever, with fear of death**, *throughout all their life, were subjects of bondage,*

> **Hebrews 2: 14-15 YLT**

The foundation of this world is built on the fear of death. The writer in Hebrews clearly describes what happened to death and the fear of it upon His resurrection. Jesus destroyed not only death but the devil, but unless you believe that your life will be no different than the rest of the world.

Fig. 11 - Virtual Reality

Think of your world as a "bubble" formed by your personality, which is created from the darkness of this world and your subconscious programing. Your "bubble" or world echoes your beliefs, thoughts, and perceived images and offers a false sense of security as protection.

Perhaps, more importantly the world we create exalts our image and insulates us from those who may challenge our identity.

The power of our world or "bubble" is defined by our personal reality, which forms our personality. We are conditioned by fear to protect our image and pursue those with greater status or position. All of the objects and characters in our "bubble" are part of the "virtual reality" we believe to be real.

Our virtual reality is like a computer game or motion picture. Our thoughts and beliefs produce the script and determine both the characters and their roles. We are both the actor and victim of our film and believe everything that is happening is both real and outside our control.

The bubble we create operates with the same authority given to Adam when he named the animals. In other words, if we believe "the world we create" to be real, it responds accordingly.

Fig. 12 - Our World as a Bubble

People live their whole life believing they are a victim to the circumstances and conditions of the world they create. They are addicted to the drama even when it is detrimental to their well-being.

All of this occurs because of the authority we give to the unconscious program controlling our lives. We can change the program by remaining conscious and taking responsibility for its creation. *Help Lord*

The only way to "pop" the bubble is to be reunited with our spirit through the new birth, as described in John 3. Reality is found inside our spirit not in the shadows of our world.

A. IMAGES FROM A SHADOW

For the law, having a shadow of the good things to come, and not the very image of the things, can never with these same sacrifices, which they offer continually year by year, make those who approach perfect.

Hebrews 10:1 NKJ

Man was made in the image of His Creator, but his sin made him a shadow. He was no longer an image of the true *Light*, but even worse he became a shadow. This is why man is afraid of *light* and chooses to live in darkness. (John 3:19)

The scripture says the Law is a shadow of the good things to come. Jesus came to fulfill the law, so He is the *Light* of the law, which produced the shadow. Jesus was the source for the law.

Until Jesus entered the earth, miraculously, as God's Lamb, the access to the Father was limited mainly to Israel through the Law of Moses. **Do not ever be confused, the Bible is entirely about the Law being resurrected into the Christ.** Therefore, it is not about Israel, David, Moses, or Abraham but rather Jesus becoming the Christ.

The soul or sin consciousness is the source of light or wisdom in this world system. The Law was the tool God used to expose the sin consciousness of man to the true Light of Christ and destroy satan's rule over mankind.[2]

Here is what I want you to see, the law was the shadow of Jesus not the source of power. Therefore, all religious systems are shadows ministering to shadows.

The scriptures in John tell us Jesus was the Life and *Light* for mankind. Thus, Jesus paid the supreme price as the sacrificial lamb to redeem the souls of man and free all those who were In Him before the foundation of the world.

Those who follow religious systems are satisfied with the wisdom from this world, because all religions are from the souls of men, whose light is darkness. The Old Covenant did not present an image of God but rather a shadow from the physical body of Jesus of Nazareth.

We define the transition between the Old and New covenant as the law becoming the resurrected Christ.

Matthew, Mark, Luke, and John the four Gospels as they are called are not the New Testament as Bibles indicate, but rather the account of Jesus fulfilling the law and the prophesy made in Genesis. The entire Old Testament was the historical account of that coming event.

_____

2 For more illumination on this subject read my book The Last Adam

And I will put enmity between you and the woman, and between your offspring and her Offspring; **He will bruise and tread your head underfoot,** *and you will lie in wait and bruise His heel.*

Genesis 3:15 AMP

The Messiah's birth, death, and resurrection are clearly prophesied, recorded, and fulfilled in the scriptures and in fact, it is the only prophesy that matters. Why?

Because the fulfillment of that prophesy, which is the resurrection, completely changed both the material and spiritual laws that controlled mankind since his expulsion from the garden of Eden.

This scripture below illustrates the transition that was occurring planetarily after the resurrection of Christ. The kingdom of God was reestablished as the new Jerusalem, which is the warfare written about in Revelation and Peter.

But the day of the Lord will come like a thief. On that day the heavens will pass away with a dreadful noise, **the elements will be consumed by fire, and the earth and all the works done on it will be exposed.** *("stoicheia" Greek for rudiments[3])*

2 Peter 3:10 CEB

3 Strong concordance 4747

In essence, Christ told Peter that He was the consuming fire that had changed all things, including death and the fear of death. (Hebrews 12:29)

Jesus, the Christ, fulfilled every prophecy written and unwritten about Him and signified it by saying, on the cross, "it is finished." (John 19:30) This included redeeming all mankind before and after the flood.

If we consider the power of what Christ accomplished through His birth, death, and resurrection beyond a historical and theological interpretations our joy will be overwhelming, and we will abide in the peace that surpasses understanding. ♡ thank you

I remember as a child the emotions I felt the night before a vacation. My mind was brimming with expectations and visions of the adventures that awaited me in the upcoming trip. The emotions I experience today as a result of my experiences with the risen Christ far exceed those when I was a child.

The resurrection of Christ is the image of God that reproduces sons of resurrection on the earth. In addition, His resurrection cleaned and redeemed all dimensions visible and invisible. This was the plan from the beginning between the Godhead and all of us who were in Him before the foundation of the world.

The resurrection is the true image of God and the fulfillment of all the scriptures. But if your focus is on verses that speak about Israel before Christ, you will conclude that the Messiah has not come. Moreover, you will be confined by the shadows of the law and live with feelings of condemnation.

having a form of godliness but denying its power. Have nothing to do with such people.

2 Timothy 3:5 NIV

The image of a shadow is the form of godliness without power or substance. The majority of the people in religious settings love the form of religion but are afraid of the substance because they have not experienced His resurrection.

The current conditions throughout the planet reflect the unbelief and fear promoted by religions of the western world. Moreover, most Christian churches show the image of a dead Jesus on the cross and quote scriptures that do not exalt the resurrected Christ.

There are many who identify themselves as prophets and proclaim future events of gloom and doom. Do not be fooled by the titles of these people because they are not acquainted with the resurrected Christ, but rather the dead Jesus on a cross.

Unfortunately, pride is the spirit that drives these people, and as mentioned in the book of Acts, it was the same spirit that killed Stephen after he spoke about destroying their temples.

All religious systems build their foundations on false doctrines because there is no substance in shadows. Before you believe "prophetic words" ask yourself if the prophesy is from the shadow or the image?

Christ upon His resurrection gave the keys to His Church, but religion will always stand in the way just like it did during His time. The church has always had the keys to the kingdom, but because they chose to eat from the tree of knowledge, there will be nothing new under the sun.

> *So, religious scholars, judgment will come on you! You're supposed to be teachers, unlocking the door of knowledge, and guiding people through it. But the fact is, you've never even passed through the doorway yourselves. You've taken the key, left the door locked tight, and stood in the way of everyone who sought entry.*
>
> **Luke 11:52 The Voice**

But here is the good news. If you believe God flooded the earth, then you must believe what Jesus did at His resurrection was more powerful. The validity of that statement is revealed in the number of days of these supernatural events.

> *Seven days from now I will send rain on the earth for forty days and forty nights, and I will wipe from the face of the earth every living creature I have made."*
>
> **Genesis 7:4 NIV**

As we mentioned earlier Christ walked the earth for forty days reestablishing the glory, which is exactly the same number of days it rained on the earth. Remember, "glory" is the word for resurrection.

After His death Jesus showed the apostles a lot of convincing evidence that He was alive. For 40 days He appeared to them and talked with them about the kingdom of God.

Acts 1:3 GW

For the earth shall be filled with the knowledge of the glory of the Lord; it shall cover them as water.

Habakkuk 2:14 Brenton Septuagint

God reveals Himself in every possible way to mankind and many times it has been through numbers. Perhaps, it is because our planet functions according to the speed of light that mathematically confines us within time and space.

The numbers are not magical but are perfect tools created by God as a signpost to those having a hard time remembering who they are in Him.

God created this material dimension for all creation to experience His glory and resurrection. Today you can exchange your image for His. How? Study the words of Jesus, whose words are spirit and life.

Most people form an image or identity from the external world and usually at some point in their life they need salvation from the image they have created. They go to a church and are introduced to an image of Jesus by their doctrines, messages, scriptures, and other people.

Now they have an image that will rescue their image. This is the result of churches who are still teaching scripture from the law because they are not acquainted with Christ.

Remember, the law crucified Jesus in order for Him to become the Christ to fulfill the following verse Hebrews.

> ***His Son is the reflection of God's glory and the exact likeness of God's being.*** *He holds everything together through his powerful words. After He had cleansed people from their sins, He received the highest position, the one next to the Father in heaven.*
>
> **Hebrews 1:3 GWT**

The resurrected Christ became the last Adam and retained the image and likeness of His Father. That is the only image we will ever need, but spoiler alert, He is imageless.

6

We are Born
FROM ABOVE

A. FREE WILL IS NOT FREE

If we believe the scriptures that describe our origin In Him before the foundation of the world our current situation should reflect that position. (Ephesians 1:4)

The only reason it does not is because we submit to the sin conscious program preinstalled into our souls. What does that mean?

The Godhead made man in their image with the freedom of choice. This was all part of the majestic plan before the foundation of the world, but it would require the ultimate sacrifice of Jesus, which was finished before we arrived in our physical body.

Nevertheless, your condition and circumstances are not what defines you. Jesus arrived and did the will of His Father's, which reestablished His kingdom. Moreover, His resurrection set us free from the consequences of our unbelief.

Unbelief created sin and corrupted the bloodline for all mankind, but the good news is the "last" Adam paid the ultimate price to redeem what was lost.

The words of Jesus are more than words because they removed the authority of sin consciousness as the only choice of mankind. Nevertheless, unless you make the choice to stop thinking and believing the lies from this world nothing will change.

Free will is free when choices arise from our origin before the foundation of the world. All choices inside the third dimension have consequences, because they were formed in duality.

Jesus preached about the Kingdom but also made a powerful declaration to go with it: He said that it required eyes to see and ears to hear. We read and hear it, but do we really understand the magnitude of that statement?

> Yet the Lord has not given you a [mind and] heart to understand and eyes to see and ears to hear, to this day.
>
> **Deuteronomy 29:4 AMP**

The system of this world is coded into our souls and minds at birth and functions like encrypted software. The result is we are both blind and deaf to the light and sound of The Spirit.

> *For this people's mind is stupefied, their hearing has become dull, and their eyes they have closed; to prevent they're ever seeing with their eyes, or hearing with their ears, or understanding with their minds, and turning back, so that I might heal them.*
>
> **Matthew 13:15 WEY**

Jesus was paraphrasing the words of Isaiah to describe the religious condition of the Jews. You may be surprised to learn that nothing, as it pertains to our birth condition, has changed from the day Jesus spoke those words.

We are born spiritually blind and deaf, and our condition will stay the same unless our thoughts change. How do you change your thoughts? You must be reborn by the water and the Spirit as explained in John 3.

It was not until I began to meditate on the following scripture that my eyes and ears were transformed.

> *Life is spiritual. Your physical existence doesn't contribute to that life. The words that I have spoken to you are spiritual. They are life.*
>
> **John 6:63 GWT**

Is it any wonder that most people who attempt to read or understand the Scriptures find it difficult? This is because we are educated and trained through our physical senses, which is not designed to discern spiritual things.

Most of what we have been taught to believe concerning the Scriptures and about our identity are inaccurate. In fact, those preconceived ideas are preventing us from freely moving between heaven and earth right now.

For example, we are taught to rely on our senses to survive much more than being guided by the Holy Spirit. There are no schools to train you spiritually inside the third dimension. Why? No one can train anyone spiritually from a dimension that is afraid of death. This is why most churches have become a business and not a school for spiritual training, which has contributed to the corruption of the gospel.

The real training occurs spiritually and that ensues each time we remove our attention from the material realm to be present in the eternal now. In order for this to happen we must live by faith instead of the laws that govern this world. This requires a thinking totally foreign to this world.

Nevertheless, our emotions and senses are used by God to create a hunger for more of Him. This usually happens after we exhaust other options, which generally introduces us to experiences with emotional trauma such as, disease, divorce, betrayal, and bankruptcy.

In other words, most people discover the

emptiness of this world before turning to the abundance inside a life of faith.

Researchers report that we are conscious of the present moment ten seconds of every minute. That means for 50 seconds we are chasing thoughts that prevent our knowing God. That condition improves as your attention increases to capture every fleeting moment.

Where we place our attention is where we spend our spiritual energy. As you study this book something will happen to you. Because you were selected In Him and are being exposed to a different light, which is removing the veil from your eyes.

We have all seen the commercials featuring "before and after" pictures of people who look or feel fabulous after using XYZ products. The "after" pictures convince us that our physical transformation is only a phone call away. Humans are born consumers and economics has taken it to the next levels.

All advertising is effective because we are taught from birth that science and technology can create something from the laboratory to improve our life. Moreover, the belief that we are material creates the insatiable desire for more to sustain and improve our life.

Nevertheless, the truth is we are born the "after," fully equipped to operate in heaven and earth, but unbelief provokes us to perceive our image as "before."

We are the "after" and do not need product XYZ from the external to improve what Christ provided at His resurrection. We must stop searching outside ourselves for treasures we already possess. Nevertheless, if we believe ourselves to be the image we see in a mirror, we will continue to look externally for solutions to our perceived problems.

The free will to choose is at the heart of every human dilemma because of the feelings of lack. The fear of not having what we may need to survive becomes a motivation for us to consume from birth to death.

The fear of death is the central driving factor that most people think about most of the time, but rarely mention in public. In fact, it is the framework for all the decisions and laws that form our world and thinking.

Therefore, the populations of the planet are continually scanning the environment for anything that is a threat to their life. In the minds of people disaster can take the form of anything unfamiliar or frightening.

In addition, most persons live their life expecting the worst possible outcome from circumstance they cannot control or foresee. This why most people repeat the same predictable behaviors and reside in the past. They figure they can't control what they have never experienced so is better to live in the past, which results in a future that resembles the past.

Therefore, people relive their past expecting the worst while hoping for a miracle. This is the mindset for people that gamble and play the lottery even though they know the chances of winning are remote. They put their faith in luck instead of the resurrection.

People gamble for the riches of this world because they believe money will protect them from their fear of death. The mentality of sin consciousness is always searching for salvation in the system that is created to steal, kill, and destroy all human beings. Whereas something as simple as believing and acknowledging the finished work of Christ will bathe you in His presence and attract His resurrection power.

Worship is not singing as much as it is tuning to the frequency of heaven and celebrating His finished work, which includes your victory over the world. We can walk in that victory by changing our attention from the external to our internal, from the physical to the spiritual.

We are all hypnotized at birth to believe and trust our senses and to follow the multitudes who have gone before us searching for the world's treasures.

This world can neither improve nor provide us with anything more valuable than that pearl that resides inside your spirit right now.

The resurrection generation are the ones who celebrate His kingdom now in the full assurance that Christ returned them to their origin. They are free from laws of this world because they are not afraid.

B. IMAGES WITHOUT LIGHT

We do have an image, but it is concealed by the image of Our Father. Meditate on the verse from Thomas below.

Jesus said, "The images are manifest to man, but the light in them remains concealed in the image of the light of the Father. He will become manifest, but his image will remain concealed by his light. "

Thomas 83 Apocryphal

The reality of who you are is the first day *Light*, which is inside our spirit, not outside in the material world. God created man complete and lacking nothing, but doubt and unbelief changed our awareness, which dimensionally altered our bandwidth.

In other words, our spiritual origin functions beyond the speed of light, which defines and restricts this dimension. Therefore, the frequencies here on earth do not compare with those of our origin.

Consequently, the light we depend on from the fourth day is destroying our spiritual understanding. This dimension and planet are but a shadow of the true light.

Each time we choose to believe images from our external or physical world we lose bandwidth or frequency that we desperately need to access the invisible realm.

Our source is *The Light* or Spirit, which makes our bodies a ground or electrical conduit for the frequency of Light. Remember, all material is formed by atoms which are pieces of energy that are more spirit than matter. Our bodies emit radiation fields, which resemble electromagnetic rings similar to those around the planet Saturn.

These light fields are both an antenna and receiver for the invisible spiritual dimensions that increase and decrease in size and strength according to what the heart and mind believe.

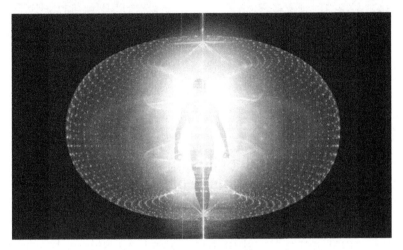

Fig. 13 - Electromagnetic field spiritually connected

Imagine yourself as a battery connected to a star that was created to shine forever. The battery is connected to God the source of all life but if that connection is broken the star will begin to die and eventually fall from the sky.

If we choose to believe the world is the source for our happiness, power, and wealth, our connection and power with the spiritual dimension diminishes. Moreover, the more we conform to the world system the more stress we experience, which drains more energy until our physical bodies deteriorate.

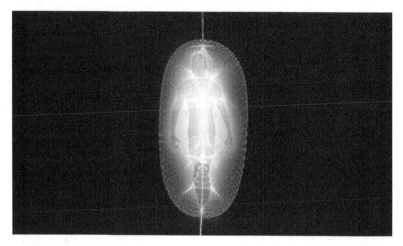

Fig. 14 - Being Physically Connected Shrinks our Electromagnetic Field

Wrong thinking and believing are the result of our separation from the source of the true *Light* of God. Therefore, our bodies are the physical reflection of what we believe. So, if we believe and are convinced, we must get a flu shot to protect ourselves from a disease, it's because we created a personal reality or personality that gets sick. That separation from the truth allows us to succumb to sickness and disease and even aging.

We are taught at birth that accumulation and consumption from the world produces happiness and success and that pressure causes people to steal, cheat, and rob. This stress is reproduced in every civilization on the earth since the fall of mankind.

In addition, the subconscious programs that drive our personalities always expect a worst-case scenario in every circumstance because of our addiction to feelings of loss, betrayal, disease, anger, and death.

However, the more acquainted you become with your spiritual nature, you will realize that your thoughts are capable of producing immunoglobulin, or IGA, which is one hundred times stronger than any flu shot.

The bottom line is this, **if thoughts can make you sick then they can also make you well.** Our singular purpose as man is to live as *The Light* in harmony with all life. This includes divine health not only for yourself but those around you.

The collective consciousness of this world is the result of darkness from the foundation of fear and death. Jesus, as The Word did not come to condemn the world but to bring *The Light* of reconciliation.

We awake each day with the same two trees that were in the original garden. Will you choose according to your senses or to the spirit? The choice we make is determined by the light we use to discern the truth.

The shadows from this dimension create images that nourish and feed our senses, which veils our eyes and ears to *The Light* of our origin.

The world eats from the tree of knowledge each time it believes the wisdom from the light in this world. Sickness, disease, the love of money, and death are the lies we believe from the understanding of this world.

The Light and The Word are One and this is our origin, and it is what illuminates and governs our thinking. If we are In Him before the foundation of the world our life is whole, not fragmented, not divided, not sick not dying not anything that darkness produces.

Therefore, when you see "wholeness" the *light* that governs you is from His Spirit. God has shown me glimpses of His Image which is formless but contains all forms.

In other words, nothing is everything when you see Him.

WHOLENESS
AND SEPARATION

A. SPIRITUAL AND PHYSICAL COMPONENTS

At an early age I remember being rebuked by my parents for going near the water for fear I would drown. My mother guarded my every move around water to protect me from her fear. The truth is babies are born swimmers and capable of being birthed underwater.

My parents were taught to be afraid of water from their parents who learned it from theirs and so on throughout the generations. Therefore, our perceptions of the environment are both mentally and physically formed from our parents and their parents before them.

Parents believe the best way to prevent disaster is to program children to be afraid. The result is most children are born into this world with the fears, beliefs, attitudes, and goals deposited like computer codes into our subconscious from the sin consciousness of this world.

By now you know that you are spirit. Moreover, you are more conscious of that reality now than when you began reading this book. But the circumstances you may be experiencing is hindering you from reentering that position In Him. Let's examine our design in order to correct anything out of order.

First read what Jesus says about the various components of man as it relates to wholeness and worship.

> *Jesus answered, "The most important is, 'Listen, Israel! The Lord our God,* **the Lord is One.**
>
> *And you shall love the Lord your God from your* **whole heart and from your whole soul and from your whole mind and from your whole strength.**
>
> **Mark 12:29-30 LEB**

The importance of God as One cannot be exaggerated because our origin was from that image and likeness.

Jesus understood the only way man can be whole is to worship in a divine sequence of heart, soul, mind, and body.

Please notice that the reason our lives are fragmented and separated from God is because our body, brain, and mind are the order we use today when we make decisions including, love.

The spirit, soul, and mind are the components designed to work in harmony with our "earth suit" called brain and body. Adam was created from the material dimension but clothed in glory. That made him one with heaven and earth.

The spirit, soul, and mind are designed to function simultaneously in both the visible and invisible arenas, while consciously observing the material world.

In other words, our spiritual components are multidimensional and not confined by the laws from this dimension. This will require your meditation to fully grasp the significance of this design. But trust me you will not be wasting your time.

> Jesus said, "Recognize what is in your sight, and that which is hidden from you will become plain to you. For there is nothing hidden which will not become manifest."
>
> **Thomas 5 (Apocryphal)**

The soul is where we build our persona or personality. This is the place we define who we are and what we believe. Jesus was very conscious of His soul because He knew that was the most vulnerable part of Adam.

It is very important for you to realize that. Before the resurrection of Christ, satan was ruling over the dimensions affecting our thoughts. This was why God flooded the earth and changed its original design.

The Bible talks about a second heaven, which in my opinion is the dimension that influences thought. His resurrection cleansed every heavenly dimension thus allowing man access to His glory and frequency.

Therefore, when he experienced emotions other than joy, He knew it was a satanic attack. In the following scripture we find satan targeting the soul of Jesus with anxiety before the cross. Look at this verse and rejoice.

> *Now My soul has become troubled; and what shall I say, Father, save Me from this hour'? But for this purpose, I came to this hour.*
>
> ***Father, glorify Thy name.***" *There came therefore a voice out of heaven: "I have both glorified it and will glorify it again.*"
>
> ### John 12:27-28 NASB

WOW!!!! If anyone understood the authority over death it was the resurrected Christ. Shouldn't we be just as confident whenever our souls are troubled? Begin now resisting fear in any shape or form and your life will be transformed.

The mind is the antenna for the soul, and it attracts the frequency equal to that of the soul.

For example, vibrations of fear activate the mind to construct a magnetic field around the body that attracts the signature of fear in the form of disease, accidents, divorce, job loss or death.

Fig. 15 - The Soul and Mind are the Antenna

The soul and mind of all mankind born into this world are servants to the sin consciousness of the world. Moreover, the majority of people or the collective consciousness of the world behaves within the sin consciousness of unbelief, fear, and death.

We are unconscious of our thoughts that are negative, fearful, homicidal, suspicious, angry, destructive, and faithless. Moreover, by the time we are 35 years old we are a programmed set of ideas, beliefs, attitudes, fears, and routines, and 95% of what we believe originated from those unconscious programs.

This means that the subconscious program of unbelief installed at birth has conditioned us to believe that what we think and believe are true and normal. The term subconscious is the mind that is asleep and functioning like an automatic pilot in an aircraft.

Our minds have been anesthetized by sin and operate on automatic pilot. The mind reproduces into the body what the soul has been programed to believe. The soul creates the frequencies, and the mind transmits the signals.

In other words, the soul of man is the center of fear and that is the vibration and frequency it produces 24/7. The mind amplifies that frequency into the body and brain, which forms the electromagnetic field around us attracting the same signal we broadcast into our world.

The brain is to the body what the mind is to the soul. In other words, if you touch a hot stove the image of pain is connected to that experience. The brain stores the images of pain associated with a hot stove as a computer file and the body produces the feeling of pain. The connection is made in the brain between the image and the feeling and over time the body can respond to the image without any physical contact with the stove.

Moreover, the brain makes the chemicals equal to the feelings released by the body. For example, if you feel sad, depressed, victimized, abandoned or lonely those feelings activate the hypothalamus in the brain that makes chemicals equal to the emotion. After a period of time, the body reacts without the chemicals of the brain making it the unconscious mind. In other words, the body responds to feelings from thought alone. This is why people can have a panic attack by thought alone.

The brain and the body are formed from the material of the third dimension, which means they are restricted by the same laws that govern all matter. **Nothing from the physical world will solve a spiritual condition.** Nevertheless, everything is connected to The Father of all Spirits. The entanglement research demonstrates that perfectly.

Many churches and religious organizations encourage their followers to enroll their children in their schools. The reason for this is to oversee the downloading of programs, so that they will be assured the child will reproduce their beliefs, attitudes, and behavior in life. This method functions to reproduce the religious systems but will not solve the sin consciousness of all those born into this world.

This is of vital importance, because those who spend their physical life becoming wise under this world's light will always be conditioned by the shadows. Remember this, as you listen to "experts" from this world who proclaim to have the answers for your life.

You are awakening now to why you experience lack, despair, and unbelief.

There is a phrase in computer technology called "wiping the hard drive". This generally occurs when a computer has a virus. Our mind had its memory wiped by a virus called sin, that arrived in the soul of all men after Adam.

But the good news is when Christ resurrected, He gave us the ability to have total recall. How? This is through His water and spirit, which results in the new birth. <u>You will know when this has occurred in your life</u>, because you will be able to worship with your heart, soul, mind, and body.

B. THE LANGUAGE OF VERBS

God made you dynamically both physically and spiritually. The word dynamic means constantly moving or in motion. For example, at the molecular level of the body we have new skin every month, a new liver every six weeks and a new stomach lining every five days, but unfortunately, the new organs will be formed according to their current condition, which is the result of what we believe. Unless I change the source of my believe, the outcome will be the same.

In other words, at the cellular level the organs and skeleton of the body changes completely every year. In fact, everything in the material world is changing, which means our language should only consist of verbs to describe our relationship with life on this planet.

Think with me for a minute. One of the first places in the scriptures that speaks about language is Babylon. Language itself was created as a means to exalt man over God. It came as a result of having joined their hearts and minds to separate themselves from their creator.

Does that mean we should be illiterate or unable to communicate? The answer is obvious, because I'm using language to write, but the power of language is greater than in the construction of sentences and education.

God speaks to us spirit to spirit and the manifestation of that communication is the faith we express through our actions. You have heard the expression "I can't hear what you say because your actions are too loud". I believe this is very true. **Our faith is the verb that illustrates that we hear God.**

Furthermore, we must embrace the unknown, because that is the location of His kingdom and our freedom. The more you understand your true self as spirit, the less attached you become to this ever-changing material world.

Our problem begins at birth because we forget our origin and begin the routine of life, which demands we find safety and security in this ever-changing planet called earth.

As you unravel the unconscious programming that has veiled your true spiritual nature you will witness a reality much greater than what we have been taught.

We are first and foremost spiritual beings not just a body and brain. We have a divine design and destiny that is beckoning us to remember that reality and origin. That journey will reconnect you with the wholeness you desperately desire.

C. THE ONENESS IN GOD

Have you ever watched hundreds of birds flying as one in enormous groups? The remarkable action of oneness occurs as they all turn at once in the same direction at the same time. My first thought is to wonder, how is it possible? Science calls this phenomena *emergence* and research shows it occurs in nature and also in our bodies.

Fig. 16 & 17 - Birds and Fish Demonstrating Emergence

The definition of *emergence* according to the Cambridge dictionary is: "The fact of someone or something appearing by coming out from behind something." In other words, both visible and invisible parts of a whole can change or transform into a shape or form spontaneously.

These types of phenomena are especially puzzling to science whose single goal is to develop models and formulas that accurately predict everything in their world. That obsession is rooted in man's fear of the unknown. The pursuit of predictability is the hallmark of science and what society desires to feel safe.

Therefore, when they discover something that is outside their ability to control or predict they quickly find a term to describe the unknown. In other words, every sickness and disease must be labeled and categorized with a name or "number." The medical profession does this all the time to convey the message of safety and placate the fear of mankind.

Nevertheless, emergence displays the "oneness" of God and it is described by Paul to demonstrate the headship of Christ inside our physical dimensions.

> *For in Him were created all things in heaven and on earth, visible and invisible. Whether they are kings or lords, rulers or powers everything has been created through him and for him. He existed before everything and holds everything together. He is also the head of the church, which is his body. He is the beginning, the first to*

come back to life so that he would have first place in everything. God was pleased to have all of himself live in Christ.

Colossians 1:16-19 GWT

The highlighted parts of the scriptures are more profound than words could describe. These verses demonstrate the overwhelming authority of Christ before creation and after resurrection.

In all things we see His headship functioning as Christ consciousness throughout all dimensions of creation. There is no doubt that when we observe nature moving as one without a visible leader it is because creation is responding to her creator.

There is nothing created by God that is above the headship of Christ. The phenomena known as emergence is just one example of God demonstrating His power and glory in the visible world.

Therefore, when we look outside ourselves it should be to see wholeness not fragments, because separation is the beginning of division and stress, which is the recipe for sickness and materialism.

Here is what I want you to read and understand. God designed us to respond to His thoughts just as effortless and natural as the birds. In fact, He says we are more valuable than the birds that He cares for with food and shelter. (Matthew 6:26)

There must be a conscious awareness of His unknowable love and grace to enter that place of rest. This is more real now than ever before. Why?

Because in this season of God's grace there is a new wind accompanying the flight of the birds and the movements of the fish. He is doing more than we can ask or imagine for this generation.

You recall in Genesis that on the fifth day He created the animals that flew and those that swim. Why is this important?

We associate the number five with the grace of God. The creatures formed on that day are God's visible sign to us of His grace. For example, the birds sing in harmony to melodies we don't know or understand. The whales and dolphins sing and move to the sounds and vibrations of the seas.

The beauty of the oceans and its creatures are portrayed and written about in countless sonnets and poems. All the creatures that navigate the heavens and the waters do so by His thoughts and perfect design.

We are helpless to comprehend the depths of God's treasures, as the son of man, but that changes after we enter His kingdom. All the mysteries of the universe are quickened inside our spirit to visibly witness the matchless grace and mercy of God. The following verse is much more powerful now that you know how He loves us.

> *Look at the birds. They don't plant, harvest, or gather the harvest into barns. Yet, your heavenly Father feeds them. Aren't you worth more than they?*
>
> **Matthew 6:26 NOG**

Once I comprehended the depths of that verse, my eyes were opened to the fact that any attempt, I could make at controlling my life was the highest form of unbelief. Why? Because God gave me His kingdom and any effort on my part to improve or control that gift disqualifies me from entering His peace.

> *Have dominion over the fish of the sea, over the birds of the sky, and over every living thing that moves on the earth.*
>
> **Genesis 1:28 WEB**

We have dominion over the birds, which means we are one with the mind of God and given the freedom to join our thoughts with His.

God does not share His secrets with those who live in separation or independence. Therefore, my trust in Him is absolute, which means I must renounce any thought that separates me from oneness.

All judgement, unbelief, doubt, fear, are forms of separation from the wholeness that make me One with Him. That conscious effort has opened the portals of heaven for me to witness His kingdom in its majestic Oneness.

My waking moments are spent in the conscious awareness that the creator of heaven and earth lives inside me. Wait a minute, you didn't hear me. God is inside me and that consciousness alone produces oneness.

Does that mean I'm conscious of that all the time? Of course not, but when that happens, I step back and breath in His mercy and grace. That act repositions me into the eternal present moment of oneness.

The separation Jesus felt on the cross is real and this is how we must defend our oneness with Him. Therefore, when you feel isolated, abandoned, fearful, or lost from Him stop and remember His resurrection.

My friend can I tell you that establishing this place IN HIM leaves no doubt that everything has been orchestrated to give Him the Glory and honor. God has left nothing to chance because of His great love towards us.

Be at peace you are exactly where you need to be to experience that great love.

D. RESURRECTION RESTORES WHOLENESS

The Bible says we are all connected to The Father of spirits because we are spirit, but our physical birth separates us from that relationship with an invisible wall that our senses cannot detect.

> On earth we have fathers who disciplined us, and we respect them. Shouldn't we place ourselves under the authority of God, the Father of spirits, so that we will live?

Hebrews 12:9 GW

The preoccupation with the material dimension compounds our separation making us forget about the oneness we once shared with our Father. We have discussed oneness as the place of peace and wisdom, nevertheless individuality is celebrated and revered in the third dimension.

As I said before, this dimension is constructed to function in duality or good and evil, which is defined by the number two. This also is reflected by the separation of the woman from the man. However, man is instructed to love the woman as himself, which is always the solution for the duality mentality. This is critical to understand.

The instant I feel separation is the moment the Holy Spirit reminds me to love what appears separate in order to reconnect with wholeness.

The resurrection of Christ is the ultimate display of that truth. Jesus separated from His Father in order to reconnect all mankind as the Christ.

All of our troubles on earth are the result of our refusal to love the perceived problem or the division we see. If you are having problems loving, it's because you haven't changed the way you think.

From then on, Jesus began to tell people, Turn *to God and* **change the way you think and act**, *because the kingdom of heaven is near!*

Matthew 4:17 GW

In order to change our thinking, we must be conscious of our thoughts. We have demonstrated our programmed thinking is the product of a sin consciousness and if we desire that to change, the first step is to stay conscious of the present moment.

All creation both visible and invisible are the thoughts of God. In fact, God says that in Jeremiah.

> *For I know the thoughts that I think toward you, says the LORD, thoughts of peace, and not of evil, to give you an expected end.*

Jeremiah 29:11 NKJ

We know that our thoughts are responsible for our condition and beliefs. Our spirit's separation from the soul and body has formed a void, which is the emptiness that reinforces the fear of death. Consequently, that separation frightens us into depending on the subconscious program that resides inside our soul.

Fear combined with the light from this dimension adds to our dependence on the subconscious programming that makes us feel more separated. Do you understand?

Remember, the peace that passes understanding is where you abide until you lose your peace with thoughts that produce separation. In other words, feelings of lack makes us look for something material to change that feeling.

We have no physical concept of our Heavenly Father, so we fill that void with physical things in our surroundings. This never-ending circle of emptiness stops after we are conscious of the present moment. The circle becomes a spiral to heaven when we stop chasing thoughts and observe them.

Our perceived separation from God is the primary reason for our fear of death and our desires for external objects to distract us, which is part of the subconscious programming.

These subconscious programs have a back door, which is computer terminology for secret entrance into a program. Your entrance into it is available each time you observe your thoughts while breathing His mercy and grace.

Our future was completed at His resurrection, which means believing what He did makes you one with His finished work. Once you are addicted to that peace, your eyes and ears will open to recognize that you never left where you originated in Him.

E. HYPNOTIZED TO BELIEVE A LIE

What if I told you we are hypnotized at birth to believe we need something from the environment to make us whole? This is why it is so imperative to awaken to the present.

The real good news is that Jesus destroyed that spell and set us free by placing everything we need in our spirit. However, our not believing that, is the sin that perpetuates the separation and why you are feeling lack, disease, or fear.

Your unbelief is the only thing that stands between you and freedom. Christ, upon His resurrection placed the keys of death and hell inside you, to ensure nothing from this world could hold you captive!

This should be extremely good news for everyone who believes they are in captivity.

We are spirit, created after the image of God to be His reflection and voice. Man was created with unique abilities to both know and think. Before Adam was separated, his spirit was connected with God to reproduce on earth His thoughts and desires.

The soul is incapable of knowing the things of the spirt because it was created to serve the spirit. You will remember that the spirit and soul vibrate at different frequencies but when they operate in the order designed by God, they are one.

All thoughts occur outside the brain and body. We are spirit and so are our thoughts, which are not confined to a physical structure.

That means if our minds are one with Christ our thoughts will reflect His Light. Therefore, in His light there are no shadows, which should deliver you from any condition associated with the fear of death.

The thoughts of our soul form our identity and personality, which validates our fears. This is why we must not identify with the thoughts and images we create from the external or physical realm.

The same thoughts lead to the same choices, which lead to the same behaviors, which produce the same emotions, which lead to the same experiences that are associated with a feeling. The endless loop of thinking and feeling forms our relationship with this world. Moreover, this becomes our state of being and forms our personal reality.

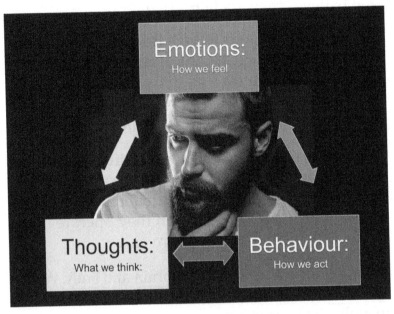

Fig. 18 - Thinking and Feeling

For example, if we get out of bed and begin thinking about an image or event that happened, we immediately leave the present moment and return to the image or emotion connected to the thought. The mind is not governed by time but rather events, which are memories from the past.

In short, you are reliving the event and producing the same chemistry associated with that experience. For example, if you are feeling abandoned by an experience that happened, your body will relive the emotional chemistry of that feeling.

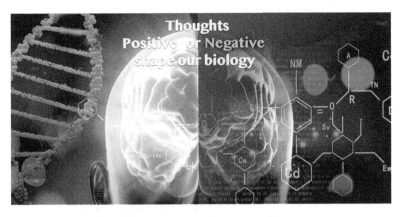

Fig. 19 - Thoughts Shape our Biology

If you keep having the same thoughts and feelings, it is unlikely anything in your life will ever change. Thus, we shape our future to replicate our past.

For, example, musical instruments not tuned properly, describe the sound of a soul whose thoughts are fearful. Noise and confusion are the sound we hear when the subconscious programs are operating inside our heads. The reason people believe their thoughts occur inside them is because of the confusion created by their souls.

If you have ever watched a horror film, you can actually feel the darkness in the scenes because technicians choreograph sounds at the infrasound level, which is below 20 hertz. These are frequencies that activate fear and produce images of darkness inside our soul.

The real scary result is that many people become addicted to that noise and drama, which reproduces imaginations associated with fear and death. Those persons become a magnet for disaster in their life and persons around them.

Wholeness occurs when the soul is servant to The Spirit, then the mind will attract the frequencies of a mind connected to heavenly frequencies.

> *and I heard a voice out of the heaven, as a voice of many waters, and as a voice of great thunder, and a voice I heard of harpers harping with their harps,*

Revelation 14:2 YLT

The description above is John's description of the sound of resurrection. Our spirit is tuned to see and hear the melody of eternal life even in the physical dimension.

God's thoughts carry a frequency of harmony and peace that can be described as the sound of many waters. Both water and light contain frequency and revelation that are critical to our physical and spiritual developments.

The conscious awareness of light and sound become the tool for attracting the sounds of heaven. Moreover, the frequencies of heaven renew your mind and body to receive revelation designed to increase our attention span to remain longer periods of time in the present moment. This is a tremendous key that has changed my life.

Observing our thoughts reveals their nature and source, which provides us with spiritual authority to select the ones beneficial for our wellbeing. The power of the elements of water and light open our understanding to why we are spirit. God's thoughts resonate with the same intensity as *The Light* from the first day of creation, when He said, Light Be. Now let me take you to a deeper understanding.

> *In the beginning the Word already existed. The Word was with God, and the Word was God. He was already with God in the beginning.*

John 1:1-2 NOG

The living water and His divine Light are both the sound and illumination of His Word. Before creation everything visible and invisible was inside His Word. The picture of that is Jesus in the flesh and the resurrected Christ.

The importance of the frequency of light cannot be underestimated especially as it pertains to our thoughts, emotions, and feelings. What we believe and perceive is the stored experiences and emotions that have shaped the way we view our world. In other words, man's thoughts are equal to the amplitude and wave of the light he perceives.

In addition, half of our memories that marked our lives are not even true. That's right, science says at least half of what we recall as a traumatic event never occurred. You are reliving events and experiencing pain of things that never even happened. Why? Because the light and frequency we use to attach images and feelings have no substance.

You may be able to see this in your life but feel helpless to change. Why? Because most people attempt to change their attitudes and perception from the same personality. The persona we form in this dimension is incapable of being anything else.

The power to change your future requires a new person, which is the description of "born again." This has become a cliché in most churches and religious settings because people are incapable of knowing the things of the spirit from a consciousness of fear.

There can be no resurrection until there is death to the personal reality we constructed from the fear of death. The baptism of spirit, soul and body defines the death and spiritual resurrection that unites us into the wholeness of The Godhead.

God is in the stillness of the unknown and no one but you can provide that atmosphere and stillness. The resurrection generation lives in wholeness and is reunited to their origin and destiny In Him.

Thoughts of life, and not death, of victory and not defeat, of greatness and not mediocracy, of unlimited glory, health, joy, and abundant peace.

Rejoice in the Lord always. I will say it again: Rejoice! Let your gentleness be evident to all. The Lord is near. Do not be anxious about anything, but in every situation, by prayer and petition, with thanksgiving, present your requests to God. And the peace of God, which transcends all understanding, will guard your hearts and your minds in Christ Jesus.

Finally, brothers and sisters, whatever is true, whatever is noble, whatever is right, whatever is pure, whatever is lovely, whatever is admirable if anything is excellent or praiseworthy—think about such things. Whatever you have learned or received or heard from me or seen in me—put it into practice. And the God of peace will be with you.

Philippians 4:4-9 NKJ

The world thrives on separation and division because they believe they must wait for something external to change them internally.

The wait ends the second you enter that generous present moment, which exposes your spirit to the oneness of your origin. If we have learned anything it is that we are One inside Christ before the foundation of the world.

The resurrection of Christ provided both the way and vehicle to live inside His kingdom now.

YOUR BODY
IS THE ARK

All of God's creations are magnificently created to both house and reflect eternity. The Old Testament ark illustrates perfectly what we are speaking about. We must become what was placed inside our spirit before the foundation of the world. You will discover a greater confidence as you complete what was finished before you were flesh.

We look away from the natural realm and we fasten our gaze onto Jesus who **birthed**

faith within us and who leads us forward into faith's perfection.

*His example is this: **Because His heart was focused on the joy of knowing** that you would be His He endured the agony of the cross and conquered its humiliation, and now sits exalted at the right hand of the throne of God!*

Hebrews 12:2 Passion Translation

There are two phrases in this translation that we should consider. Faith is the result of the resurrection because there is no reason to believe anything if death is supreme. Think of that! His resurrection is the proof that our faith is more real than what our senses reveal.

Secondly, He knew that joy is the product of knowing with our heart. **If you are not experiencing joy it is because you are believing what you see instead of what you know.**

Picture the children of Israel wandering in the dessert carrying the presence of God in a container made of acacia wood. God's people were protected from their enemies as long as they had the Ark.

The mere presence of the ark transformed the material dimension in incredible ways. For example, the clothing and shoes of the multitudes did not age for forty years nor were there any disease among the people.

The supernatural was natural for those in the vicinity of God's ark. God was believed to be inside a wood box because wherever the ark arrived the physical realm was altered.

Today, we have that same God inside our arks made of flesh, but unfortunately, we would still prefer to believe we must wait for a physical manifestation to prove His presence.

We are taught from birth to trust the physical world for our resources and protection. If you want to experience something outside this dimension that we label as a miracle or supernatural, we must start believing beyond our senses and this dimension. We have been saying this in so many different ways, but now you are awakening to the reality of the invisible.

Moreover, for hundreds of years Israel experienced no disease at all until King Asa called for a physician from the Egyptians. The people of Israel lived in divine health as long as they trusted God.

> *In the thirty-ninth year of his reign Asa was diseased in his feet, and his disease became severe; yet even in his disease he did not seek the LORD,* ***but sought help from physicians.***
>
> **2 Chronicles 16:12 NKJ**

> *"This is what the LORD says: Cursed is the person who trusts humans, who makes flesh*

and blood his strength and whose heart turns away from the LORD.

Jeremiah 17:5 GWT

The only thing that prevents us from living supernaturally is unbelief. The resurrection of Christ destroyed every enemy both physical and spiritual. Begin now to see yourself whole and refuse to believe anything that separates you from that belief.

The following section will provide more proof that what we have been taught is a lie. The truth is you arrive to this planet equipped to live in divine health.

A. EPIGENETICS DESTROYS VICTIMIZATION

Most people are taught they inherit good or bad genes, and those genes are responsible for their health and wellbeing. Science educates society to believe they are victims of genetics and helpless to the diseases or misfortunes of their bloodline. Epigenetics has shown this to be a complete and utter lie. This branch of science literally means "above" or "on top of" genetics.

Epigenetics refers to external modifications to DNA that activate genes. These modifications do not change the DNA sequence, but instead, they affect how cells "read" genes.

Genes are analogous with blueprints that architects read to construct a building. The genes are the proteins, and our minds are the architect. If our perception changes, so too does the structure of the building.

The way we perceive our surroundings, beginning inside the womb, develops us physically and mentally for our birth. After a child is born the light, sound and senses enhance the growth process, especially our eyes.

Children are exposed to the same behaviors, food, language, and culture of their parents, or whoever raise them, which means the same genes are read day after day reproducing the same images inside the mind.

You may have witnessed that after a few short years the uncanny way animals resemble their owners. This process begins with babies inside the womb and accelerate after birth. The combination of our emotions, sound, and nutrition resonates with the genes to construct the images of the environment.

The frequencies from this dimension along with our thoughts interact at the cellular level to physically shape the features and characteristics of the child.

Therefore, it is a myth to believe you are born a victim in this world because of your genetic blueprint. Much of what science has presented as doctrine and irrefutable truth is nothing more than speculation and attempts to frighten people into trusting their advice and consultation. The sooner we observe the present moment, the less attention we pay to the pseudo-science of the world.

God does not create anything but miracles. We are wonderfully created with amazing abilities to think thoughts, make a baby, play a piano, remove toxins, and react to all five of our senses simultaneously. We are created to function at much higher levels than what we are programmed to believe.

B. CELLS AND VOLTAGE

One need only to look at cells to discover the majestic way we are created. We are a composite of around 70 trillion cells that contain an electrical charge equal to 1.5 volts per cell. That is a total of 105 trillion volts of electricity that goes through our bodies carrying information vital to our physical well-being.

Every cell has consciousness, immune and respiratory systems that are a mini microcosm of the human body. Nevertheless, the lack of voltage in our cells is the number one contributing factor to disease. The body begins to die and decompose once the voltage falls below certain parameters.

For example, after researchers measured the electrical voltage of organs in the body, they determined a body was generally healthy if the voltage levels were between 75 to 90 MHz's.

The onset of flu and colds appeared in the organism when the body dropped below 50 Mhz. Moreover, diseases such as cancer and tuberculosis appeared in organs whose electrical charges dropped below 45 Megahertz.

We have explained our physical relationship to energy through atoms. We also know that our thoughts and feelings carry vibrations, which are electrical charges.

Everything in the physical dimension functions in harmony with the physical forces of voltage. Our bodies are miniature atomic reactors that require electricity to maintain harmony in the organs.

To understand this, let's take a look at plants innate ability to increase voltage and mend damaged DNA. Those of you not familiar with essential oils should get to know these miracle molecules and add it your daily routines. I fully recommend reading my book, *"The Breath of God Over Essential Oils,"* for a more in-depth study.

Each organ in the body is composed of millions of cells designed to nourish the organ with blood and light, which is the spiritual blueprint for health and healing. **In other words, lack of voltage or electrical energy results in cellular death.**

All physical disease is primarily spiritual, but at the physical level it is the result of energy deficiency. The reality is sickness and disease are the result of unbelief.

Mental stress is the fastest way to deplete the energy and leave the organs and cells defenseless against the trillions of bacteria inside the body designed to decompose the body at death.

In fact, the number one reason for 90% of doctor visits is stress related. **That and the lack of physical nutrition increases the levels of physical pain that make remaining focused on the present moment nearly impossible.**

Nevertheless, there are many people who love the Lord

but as a result of trusting their subconscious programs are having physical problems and conditions. This is written to supply you with the information you need to change the way you think and believe so you can correct your physical condition.

Have you ever noticed fungus spores on a tree leaf? They lie dormant until the tree enters a seasonal death stage that is marked by a decrease in sunlight or electrical charge, in the form of photons. This loss of voltage awakens the spores to actively change the leaf into both humic, and fulvic acid, which is composed of vitamins, minerals, and amino acids.

The soil reproduced by the dying leaves under a tree makes the perfect womb for seeds. The soil contains fulvic acid, which opens the membrane of the seed to receive the nutrients of the humic acid. If the proper water and sunlight are available, the new plant will be provided with all the natural chemistry to reproduce life in every creature that eats from the new plant.

Now, you eat the plant and receive all the nutrients including the fulvic acid that unlocks your cells to restore health and build immunity against death. Voltage is produced with the interaction of acid and alkaline in our bodies. That process is destroyed when pesticides are sprayed into the environment because it kills the humic acid.

Farmers add fertilizers that contain nitrogen, phosphorous, and potassium to make their crops grow. Unfortunately, food grown under these conditions do not supply humic and fulvic acid the cells require for healthy growth. The result is our immune system is compromised and the body's voltage will not prevent the fungi and bacteria inside our body from awakening and decomposing our bodies.

This also occurs with a process called pasteurization. The modern medical approach to disease is antibiotics, which is added to the foods we eat, which is the recipe for disease and death.

The understanding of voltage will increase your desire for natural sunlight, spring water and the company of other healthy human beings. These are simple things we can do to provide enormous amounts of energy that recharge depleted cells. This is why God put man in a garden and called it Eden.

Man was created with the innate ability to heal and reproduce after its kind. This is possible because we are created from the same earth we were instructed to dominate. This is critical to understand for you to change your thinking and believing.

Ask yourself if God would allow something in the earth that could annihilate His creation? The answer is obviously no. The fear and panic of a "virus" is a sure sign that people don't know the love of God and would rather trust man than their creator.

Your greatest opportunity for transition into authority begins after you understand the birth, death, and resurrection of Christ. The power of what Christ did at resurrection is so overwhelming and complete, that words can never describe the fullness of His actions.

The next section will provide more spiritual truths that will arm you against the lies from this world.

C. ORIENTING RESPONSE

Science divides brain wave activity according to frequency and chemistry. For example, during busy times of the day the brain is said to be in Beta. After we slow down the brain goes from Beta to Alpha. The Alpha state resembles a hypnotic condition in which a person is easily controlled with suggestions. Psychologists use a term called "orienting response" to describe a brain in Alpha state. For example, after a person sits down in front of a TV, the brain enters the Alpha or "hypnotic state", which makes it easier to program during this condition.

This is important to remember the next time you relax in front of a TV while someone tells you about a disease or disaster that could affect you. If you are not careful you will be hypnotized into believing whatever it is they are saying.

The basic needs of the body for survival are oxygen, water, sleep, and food. Animals and humans are easily conditioned to respond a certain way by using suggestions paired with the basic needs of humans. This helps us understand when we are most vulnerable to suggestions. For example, most wars are said to have been consummated over dinner and wine.

One of the best know examples of this is Ivan Pavlov who conditioned Russian wolf hounds with food to salivate to the sound of a bell. The study demonstrated the power of conditioning the body with an outside stimulus.

A human body can be conditioned to manifest cancer from suggestion, in the same way dogs are conditioned to unconsciously salivate to the sound of bells. If a person believes they are vulnerable to a disease they will unconsciously believe the suggestion and produce chemistry, which will manifest that belief in the body.

It is important to understand that suggestions and belief create electromagnetic frequencies that attract matter equal to the image. For example, when we think about sickness, we create a magnetic field that attracts images equal to the emotional wave lengths of our beliefs.

In other words, if we believe we are vulnerable to a disease such as cancer, that thought will manifest materially into our body. Remember, we spoke about changing energy into matter called collapsing the wave. This is exactly the process we invoke with our thoughts.

The first thing most people do every morning is reach for their morning fix by plugging into the worlds operating system, called the world wide web. All the devices we use in our daily lives, such as, smart phones, and computers, send images all the time, which are suggestions for us to believe.

Most people are very receptive and easily conditioned to believe the signals being transmitted, because these images and thoughts produces adrenalin and other addicting chemicals that makes us feel alive. This is compounded today by social media, because people are reinforced to believe a certain way from a simple "like" of a comment they post.

Over time the brain is incapable of producing enough chemicals to satisfy our cravings, which drives people to explore the darker regions of gambling or pornography to find the needed rush.

We are conditioned from an early age to find our happiness and wealth in the material world. You must be aware of this because the more dependent you are on digital devices and media platforms the easier you will be controlled by frequencies of fear. We must unplug from the frequencies of the world and remain in the peace and stillness of the present moment.

D. WHOSE VOICE DO YOU HEAR?

The real "Church "of the New Testament formed in the image of Christ demonstrated power over sickness, disease, poverty and even death, because the sheep were taught to hear the voice of The Good Shepherd.

> *My sheep hear My voice, and I know them, and they follow Me. I give eternal life to them. They will never perish, and no one will snatch them out of My hand.*
>
> *My Father who has given them to Me is greater than all. No one is able to snatch them out of My Father's hand. I and the Father are One."*

John 10:27-30 WEB

The Bible is clear that Jesus is The Good Shepherd of His sheep not a doctor wearing a white coat. The scripture also emphatically says that His sheep know Him by His voice. His voice is the frequency of resurrection and fearlessness over the circumstances of this world.

Awakening to that reality dramatically changes our perception and faith. Nothing is impossible because of resurrection, but each of us must "know that" in our hearts and minds. Otherwise, we will experience life from the teachings of the Old Covenant. That means we will operate under the law of good and evil waiting on a Messiah. That may sound ridiculous, but it is what the church of the last several hundred years has been teaching.

We have reached a crossroad that will define future generations. Either we will bow to the idol of Nebuchadnezzar, in the form of science, or we truly enter the kingdom of God by dying to this world system.

That may sound to challenging for those who have not been trained to understand their spiritual nature but for you who believe you were chosen before the foundation of the world it is exactly what you have been waiting to hear.

In fact, many of you have known for some time that something is not right. Be assured you are not alone. There are multitudes being stirred by a new frequency and light.

THE EXTERNAL
WORLD
IS THE PLACEBO

The term placebo has been around since the 1700's and as you will discover it is much more than just a sugar pill or inert drug. Physicians and drug manufactures know that human beings are innately capable of healing without drugs. But in order to measure the effect of their manufactured drug they test it against a non-drug called a placebo.

Before a drug is approved by the FDA, researchers are required to use methodologies of double and triple-blind studies. This means that neither the subjects nor scientist know who is getting the drug or the placebo.

The outcome from most of these studies leaves no doubt that people's belief is the drug, and the disease is the placebo. In other words, what you believe is more powerful than any disease.

In a study for depression 83% of the patients that took the placebo were immediately better than those taking the antidepressant drug. That means four out of five people were actually better than those who took the pharmaceutical medication. What does that mean?

Those taking the placebo were convinced beyond any doubt that it would cure them from depression. The belief alone activated their faith to chemically produce dopamine, and serotonin that changed their condition. Thus, the body produces better and safer chemicals than the synthetic drugs from pharmaceutical manufacturers.

In another study a man was feeling ill and went to his local doctor. The doctor sent him to a specialist who determined he had advanced stages of cancer and sadly announced he had a short time to live. The patient was reported to have told his doctor he was okay with dying as long as he could survive through Christmas to be with his family. On New Year's Day, a week after Christmas, the man died. The following week at the autopsy it was discovered the man never had cancer.

Think about that! The man surrendered, accepted, and believed what his doctor told him, which is the same way a person reacts to a hypnotist. A person that wishes to be hypnotized must be suggestible to the ideas and thoughts from a person he/she trusts.

If you have watched a drug commercial on television, you will understand the process is to first make you believe you are a victim to the disease they are selling so you will buy their cure.

The process for sickness and disease is always the same and it begins with a feeling, which leads to thoughts. In other words, how you feel becomes the way you think, which is to entertain the idea that a certain disease "could" infect you.

This is the process a farmer uses when he plants a seed in his field. The farmer waters and fertilizes the seed, which is what our thoughts and feelings do in our body. After you have convinced yourself that you have a disease you must then consult a physician to validate all of the symptoms you have created.

In Japan, a group of children with known allergies to poison ivy participated in the following. Researchers took leaves that resembled poison ivy and told the children it was the plant and rubbed it on their arms, even though it was not poison ivy the children broke out with the rash. Next, they administered the actual leaves of poison ivy and told them it was from a plant that only resembled it, and they did not react. Why?

The children's belief overrode their physiological responses to the plant. The body made the histamines necessary to counteract the effect. The thought alone made them immune.

Ask yourself right now, were you created to be a victim? The external or physical world will respond to what you believe, so, if you want a different outcome, it will require a different belief. The power of changing your thoughts begins and ends inside the present moment.

Turn your attention away from anything and everything that creates fear in your life. When we understand that His resurrection is our authority, we will overcome the fear of death and never be a victim again.

There are studies of surgeons in the war that did not have morphine for surgeries and devised a convincing argument along with his nurses to persuade the patients that the medications they would receive would be more potent than morphine and that they may feel different at first, but that the operations would be painless.

The results were astounding. The patients were given no anesthesia during the operations and 75% of the patients felt no pain. The belief the patients put in the doctors created enough morphine in their bodies to allow the surgeries with no pain.

The latest data reports that Parkinson's disease is the result of the bodies inability to make dopamine. There was a study that reported doctors telling their patients that they would receive a drug that would cure the disease. Each of the patients received the placebo drug described as the cure. The following week over 50% of the patients no longer exhibited the symptoms of the disease.

In fact, when they looked at the brain scans from the patients with no symptoms, they discovered that they had manufactured their own dopamine and, in some cases, it was two hundred times above normal. Those patients were cured from Parkinson's disease with a sugar pill because they believed and trusted the word of a physician.

It was not until the patients went home and returned to familiar surroundings and people, that the disease returned. Why? The same belief that made the dopamine and cured their symptoms is the same belief that created the disease in the first place. What do I mean?

A placebo is effective because people surrender and believe the word of the doctors. If you go to a physician, and after an exam, he or she says with conviction that you have cancer, several things happen instantly.

First, the sound and visual picture of death instantly releases "*cortisol*" that shuts down the immune system. The image coupled with the belief of death manifest materially in the body to validate the prognostication of the doctor.

This is to say that our bodies respond to what we believe and we create both our world and physical condition through our belief. We have been saying that in so many ways that it should be obvious that your body is the same as your world.

Our beliefs are from the soul, which is preprogrammed by a consciousness of sin. Therefore, unless we change programs through a spiritual rebirth our conditions will resemble what the soul believes.

The image of a doctor delivering the traumatic news is the picture that becomes both a memorial and foundation for our demise. This and other scenarios like it are all possible because we are programmed to believe our external world is more real than our creator. We may tell ourselves that we do not think that, but if you are not practicing His presence chances are your response to a similar prognostication would be very similar.

The placebo is effective for many reasons but mainly because of the belief that we require a remedy from the physical realm to heal our physical bodies.

We begin at an early age to expect sickness, disease, marriage failure, and unhappiness from the external. The study of placebos proves that our mind is the active substance that acts on the invisible realm to produce a physical manifestation.

We know by now our body is an extension of the world we create from our beliefs and perceptions. The same belief that forms our world is capable of creating the disease we manifest. Thus, if we are the author of what we experience, and we are, then why not create heaven on earth?

The fear of death will dominate the emotions and thoughts of those whose state of being is a reflection of the physical world. **We create our personality from our personal reality.** In other words, what we think is the foundation of what we believe.

Most people who come to Christ attempt to change their thinking and feeling as the same person or personality. This is impossible and it is why many people believe they need deliverance.

You can confess or make all the positive affirmations you want but if your feelings and emotions are grounded in the perceptions from this world, your body and mind will be divided. For example, if you think about divine health and abundance but your heart feels betrayed, abandoned, alone, and poor, the result will not be positive.

Jesus said a house divided will not stand, which means, if your heart and mind are not one in Him, then separation will be the result. This is at the heart of what we are writing about isn't it?

The power of medicine, religion, governments, and science is the same as a placebo. If we believe the story surrounding the subject, our body will manifest the belief. The only solution for a physical malady is found in resurrection because that requires a death to our identity with this world.

The resurrection of Christ is your personality and personal reality and that requires experiencing what you fear most, death. Remember, physical death is inevitable and painless but I'm speaking of death to your personal reality.

A placebo reveals that our trust in the material world's cure activates our faith to produce a miracle. However, we can reproduce the supernatural on earth by living inside His Kingdom now.

We are the gods of our life on this planet. In fact, David and Jesus speak about it in the Bible.

> I said, "You are gods, sons of the Most High, all of you;
>
> **Psalm 82:6**

> Jesus answered them, "Is it not written in your Law, 'I said, you are gods'?
>
> **John 10:34**

We are created in perfection through Him who chose us before the foundation of the world. The truth of that reality must be discovered individually. This is not a doctrine or theology but the spiritual substance of our image from our Father. He formed us after Himself and supplied everything we would ever need inside our spirit. In order to access that divine supply, we must not lose track of the present eternal moment. That is where our true identity is and your victory over death.

A. ADDICTED TO FEAR

I remember going to our family doctor for a sore throat and given an antibiotic to kill the infection or germ called streptococcus. All parents are trained to take their children to a physician for every ache, pain, and vaccination. These habits originated because of the planetary belief that germs are the deadly enemy of mankind. Moreover, the message has intensified because of the proclamations from science that viruses threaten to eradicate the human species.

That may seem like an overstatement until you consciously observe how much time you spend evaluating the way you feel. You would be shocked to learn the amount of unconscious energy people spend worrying about potential conditions that "could be" life threatening.

For example, you may rub your hand across your arm and notice a bump or an unusual color, which immediately creates a host of images and sensations. The mental response, nine times out of ten are pictures of a worst-case scenario.

This reaction produces stress hormones, which shuts down the immune system of the body. Disease originates after the chemistry of our brain creates a "fight or flight" condition, which compromises the immune system and devastates our physical bodies.

The unfolding drama resulting from fear will chew up hours of speculations and google searches until some thing or someone convinces you otherwise. All of this is the result of leaving the present moment to chase a thought, feeling or emotion created inside your brain. You waste time trying to discover a remedy for a disease that has no reality in the spiritual dimension.

That's right there is no disease or sickness where the "real you" originates. But if you persist in believing you are flesh, then you have created the perfect medium for a disease to prove your suspicions correct. How bad do you want to be right? That is the question each person must ask because most people want to be right even if it causes them pain. I'm reminded of the proverb that says pride goes before destruction.

The idea of evolution, although not accepted in "Christian" circles, is most certainly unconsciously believed by those who run to the physician for all their aliments. Because if we believe we evolved, then something greater than man can evolve in the form of a virus. Therefore, the population of the world believe the lie that we are the product of evolution and therefore, victims as human beings.

Do not be condemned because you are a current patient of a doctor. I believe doctors serve a valuable role in society as it pertains to treating accidents or emergencies. I know many good physicians that care about their patients and provide a valuable service. God is using some physicians to treat diseases with heavenly understanding and the wise use of natural remedies. The physician that creates the atmosphere of peace in the minds of his patients allows the Holy Spirit access to their real conditions.

The problem with good medical practitioners is the same as good minsters. Most of the people who go to churches or medical offices are spiritually asleep and looking for third dimension advice to give them a temporary solution to their spiritual condition. In other words, most people want a list of things to do to get a result rather than take responsibility for their beliefs.

Unfortunately, most physicians prescribe antibiotics that treat symptoms by killing bacteria both diseased and healthy. Antibiotic is defined as, tending to prevent, inhibit, or destroy life. Using that class of drugs is tantamount to spraying pesticides on your garden.

According to Dominique Tobbell the discovery of penicillin accelerated development of therapeutic, so-called "ethical drugs" available only by prescription. The total revenue share from prescription drugs increased from 32% of all drugs (including over-the-counter varieties) in 1929, to 83% by 1969.

We can be sure those percentages are much higher today given it is relatively impossible to watch TV for ten minutes without being bombarded with drug commercials of one kind or another. The pharmaceutical industries spend billions of dollars on these Hollywood productions to convince you that without their product you will fall prey to the malady.

The objective of these advertisements is to mesmerize the viewer into believing and reproducing the symptoms of the disease they are promoting. That's right, they are hypnotizing you to believe and manifest the sickness that their product is designed to cure. That sounds ridiculous, but it is diabolical and true.

My purpose is to remind you that Christ lives inside you. If you remain conscious of that, no disease will resonate inside the body.

B. THE SECRET OF THE TONSILS

God created our body with the innate ability to heal itself from anything external. Our tonsils, for example, are designed to sample invisible organisms that enter the body through the "holes" in the face. Our eyes, mouth, nose, and ears are the gateway to our physical organism, but the majestic design of God uses these orifices to collect invasive antigens unfamiliar to the immune system.

The immediate response of the tonsil is to both learn the character of the foreign bacteria and then build antibodies that attach to the antigen and flush it out of the system.

The antigens activate our autonomic nervous system to create powerful glycoprotein molecules called immunoglobulins or IGA, or white blood cells. They identify the foreign substance and bind to it aiding in their destruction.

History reveals that during the early 1900's, as many as 8,000 students a year, in the United Kingdom, had their tonsils removed. There is no telling how many worldwide performed this procedure. Why is this important?

I personally believe many of the "so called" viruses that required vaccinations such as polio, mumps, measles etc. are the result of improper disposal of human waste and the widespread tonsillectomies that were performed in the world as early as the 1800's.

If the number one defense against disease is removed, the result is worldwide sickness and death. Add to that the thousands of people that moved to cities that had poor or nonexistent sewer systems to adequately remove the human waste and worldwide pandemics will be the result. God made it a priority in His law to dispose of human waste properly. (Deuteronomy 23)

Worldwide disease and so-called pandemics are the result of mass numbers of people who are both spiritually and physically compromised. This is the condition of society whose trust is in the science and wisdom from this world.

Synthetic drugs or a vaccine can temporarily provide relief to a dying body because it acts the same as jumper cables for dead car batteries. The voltage from the cables will start and run the engine for a period of time but eventually the battery will have to be replaced. Physically we must rely on the Spirit of God for the right decisions as it pertains to wisdom.

Vaccines do not prevent disease it provides a synthetic chemical that the dying body could not manufacture. The lie is that it stops the disease, it does not. But you ask why do so many people "get well" after taking a vaccine or medication? The answer to that question was addressed in the chapter discussing the placebo.

Most people have relied on drugs to change their physical condition instead of providing the nutrition needed for a strong immune system. Today there is no need for tonsillectomies because the medical profession has convinced the masses that without their vaccines life on this planet would be over.

Moreover, the real danger with injecting vaccines of any kind is that the body may not recognize the drugs and shuts down. Our bodies use tonsils to defend against antigens and vaccines bypass that process.

The solution for disease begins and ends with our belief. After we are connected with our spirit, both the mind and body operate as one with our physical surroundings producing divine health. Remember, our thoughts and cells depend on voltage, which create either healthy or unhealthy conditions in our body.

Physical decay begins in our bodies the same way leaves fall off a tree during autumn. The decrease of sun or voltage creates death, but in the spring, life returns with the frequency of light. We are designed to live in a resurrection state year around because we are not subject to the laws governing this dimension.

Moreover, when we no longer fear death, we will no longer trust anyone but our creator. The medical professionals are not evil, but they are called "practicing" physicians for a reason.

God created you and He provided everything we would ever need before we were flesh and blood. Therefore, we are spiritually created to generate all the voltage we need to provide nutrition and energy to our physical bodies. The question we must answer is can we think greater than we feel? The answer to that question is emphatically yes!

C SUPERNATURAL REALITY

Our reality is formed by our thoughts and they comprise 90% of what we physically experience in our known world. Does this mean God will not physically alter the material dimension? No, we have all witnessed miracles.

We describe a miracle as supernatural because our realities and beliefs are from this world, which is labeled as normal. We should not be surprised by the extraordinary because the spiritual dimension is our normal.

There have been many situations in my life that demonstrated His attention to my most insignificant desires. For example, I recall losing a small screw that I needed to fix a chair that I enjoyed sitting in during worship.

One morning, as the memory of the missing screw crossed my mind, I looked down to discover the lost screw. The amazing thing was I found the screw in the same place I looked the day it was lost.

The joy that filled my heart so profoundly at that moment was not because I found the screw but because I felt the love of God. I knew nothing escaped His attention and, in that instant, I felt a oneness that made me forget about anything in this dimension. In other words, my attachment with this world literally disappeared.

When we know how much we are loved we can believe for anything. It was at that instant I knew what Jesus meant when He said nothing was impossible if you can believe. From that day forward it became easier to remain in the eternal present moment. Why? I learned the meaning of what Jesus told His Father in the following verse:

> *Father, I want those You have given to Me to be with Me, to be where I am. I want them to see My glory, which You gave Me because You loved Me before the world was made.*

John 17:24

Those words are timeless because He spoke them from eternity, in the presence of His Father, while He was still on earth. In other words, He reproduced the same atmosphere as He did on the mount of transfiguration. He opened the portal of His resurrection, which is His kingdom and spoke face to face with His Father.

This is available for you every time you enter the timeless present moment. Because outside time and space is where resurrection occurs, and all our perceived problems happen when we remain in this dimension.

Our biggest challenge is our preoccupation with predicting and controlling our life instead of making the time or effort to spend time in the present moment thanking Him for what He has finished.

Moreover, our obsession with the material dimension as our resource for satisfaction and sensory pleasure has confined us to dwell inside the prison of our senses.

The power of knowing the resurrected Christ changes our attention from the natural to the spiritual, which will reveal a reality much greater and more relevant than what we imagine in this world. This is because our current reality is formed in this limited dimension, which is established by the fear of death.

His bodily execution and resurrection were the last physical action required to open our spiritual eyes and ears and set us free from this dimension of time and space. This must be our conscious reality 24/7 if we want to be free from the quicksand of doubt and unbelief.

Our preprogramming and conditioning to trust the external world is learned, which means it can be unlearned. The same faith you use to believe externally can be used internally to open your eyes and ears to His Kingdom.

You were created whole and complete with the full authority to create what you need physically from your spirit.

After you discover the reality of yourself as spirit your attention to the present moment will increase and ultimately open a door to the supernatural.

The choice is yours; it's always been that way!

10

SCIENCE
AND THE
TOWER of BABYLON

Science and religion have vehemently opposed one another's ideas throughout history, but none more violently than creation. Science sided with Charles Darwin and his book, "The Descent of Man" published in 1871 that describes man's relationship to primates, but Darwin stopped short of declaring man evolved from Apes. He left that to the 20th century scientists who used their findings in DNA as proof that all life, including man, are the product of evolution.

The false belief that genetics determines our future is taught in all education systems around the world. That belief makes it easy for man to trust science more than God. Afterall, if we are victims of our genes it would seem only logical that science has the solutions for our helpless conditions.

Thus, science and all its branches, including medicine, have established themselves as the god of this universe and require all nations and peoples to submit to their wisdom and knowledge.

We are witnessing the resurrection of Nebuchadnezzar in the form of science demanding you to bow to their wisdom. This coronation has erected "science" as the new tower of Babylon for all creation to serve.

From the beginning of this decade, we have witnessed persons on every continent hiding like animals from a perceived enemy called COVID. In addition, anyone who questions the authority or methods of science and governments have been labeled a menace to society and shamed into silence and submission.

Those who believe in this system are forced to learn the language and wisdom of Babylon to live in their false sense of security and safety. Babel is broadcasting the messages of fear into the hearts and minds of those who have pledged allegiance to science as their god.

The most recent transmission is labeled COVID 19, and it reinforces the world's narrative that humans are helpless victims born into a hostile environment that will eradicate their species, unless modern science produces the cures in the form of pharmaceuticals and vaccines.

The hidden message is that mankind's only hope is that science and medicine find the solution for all the worlds ills. This terrifying image of fear has succeeded in controlling the narrative and brain washing its inhabitants.

The medical profession is the most powerful voice on the planet, which is proved by observing how they have frightened the population to believe God's creation is no match for invisible germs, viruses, or disease.

Nevertheless, they cannot and will not produce a vaccine for the plague called the "fear of death," because it is the cornerstone for the world. But they will inoculate you against the flu, so you feel well enough to fear death again. Are you seeing the total nonsense of this world system yet?

It reminds me of the "science fiction" movies depicting Martians arriving to destroy earth. The only solution to save the earth was to bring in the combined forces of military and science to battle against the invading aliens.

Notice the genre of these films are called "science fiction" because all science that promotes itself as our salvation is fiction.

This decade will be like no other for many reasons, but perhaps none more important than governments learning how to control the populations without starting a world war or firing a single shot. Not since the world wars has the voice of fear been so united to motivate billions of people to hide from an enemy that was not a country such as Germany or Russia.

Science is in complete control of the masses who are running like sheep to the slaughter with little more than the proclamation by physicians that testing positive to a virus is a death sentence.

This hour is unique for many reasons but none more profound than the number of people who profess to trust Jesus but believe the message of fear over the salvation of God. This surely reminds us of the scriptures that describe God separating the wheat from the tares.

A. GERMS AND VIRUSES

The fundamental belief in the earth today that germs and viruses are lethal, and we are helpless victims began from the false interpretations of Louis Pasteur. This lie, even when proven wrong, created the dogma whose goal is to control the world's population with fear and pharmaceuticals.

This decade has provided both the technology and the platforms to effectively deliver their messages of fear and death. Today governments can instantly transmit data throughout the various platforms of Facebook, Twitter, and cable news outlets. The voices and pictures of worldwide death are shrouded in peace and safety and delivered by our "trusted" physicians to emphasize the horror they have been tasked to save us from.

Major cities closed, including churches even though research shows that wearing mask and hiding from a germ is useless. According to Wikipedia by April 2020, half of the world's population was under lockdown, with more than 3.9 billion people in more than 90 countries or territories having been asked or ordered to stay at home by their governments.

The outcome yielded the results that oligarchies of big tech, pharmaceutical manufactures and governments had hoped to achieve. Not since Nimrod and the tower of Babel have the peoples of the planet been so united in their belief that man is their savior.

The original tower was destroyed, and their languages confused because man was united in heart and mind. Man exalting himself above his creator, repeats itself again and again throughout history.

In the scripture below we find the word imagination, which means image used in describing man's wickedness.

> *The Lord saw that the wickedness of man was great in the earth, and that every **imagination and intention** of all human thinking was only evil continually.*
>
> **Genesis 6:5 AMP**

You notice in that verse that God got involved because man's heart and mind were one. **If our heart and mind are united our language will also be one. That language will always be faith.**

Nevertheless, mental, and physical confusion will always be the result of those who attempt to live their life without recognizing Christ as Lord. Moreover, their heart and mind will also be fragmented and separate.

Before the resurrection, the thoughts and desires of man were controlled by satan who ruled from the second heaven. God protected His Son's bloodline after the flood throughout the Bible. The events of the Tower of Babel were an example.

Do I think God is going to destroy the earth? Absolutely not! But perhaps you understand why most doctrines of the churches don't comprehend what Christ accomplished at His resurrection. Why? Because countless "modern day prophets" are using current events as proof the world is about to be destroyed.

You must know that His resurrection destroyed satan and removed his authority from the second heaven, but if you don't believe that then your life will be no different from those who lived in the Old Covenant.

The conditions happening in the world today is to help us change our focus and perceptions from this limited material dimension to His unlimited supernatural Kingdom. The current situation on the planet is necessary for many reasons, but most importantly it is happening to remind us of our origin and nature.

We are in the world but should not be of it. The Israelites left Egypt, but the reason they all died in the wilderness is because the belief systems of Egypt remained inside them.

There is no returning to Egypt, or anything related to this world system. There is no compromise with a system whose purpose is to destroy you. You do realize, that don't you?

This pertains to the belief that governments of this world are somehow picked by God to rule over man. That doesn't mean good people are not in government. We know many believers that are being used by God, but they would be the first to tell you God is the authority not government.

Nevertheless, many people confuse God's kingdom with the politics of this world. That belief is wrong and condemns you to live in the old covenant. We are given the power and instructions to enter His kingdom now.

> *"My kingdom," replied Jesus, "does not belong to this world. If My kingdom did belong to this world, My subjects would have resolutely fought to save Me from being delivered up to the Jews. But, as a matter of fact, My kingdom has not this origin."*
> **John 18:36 WEY**

Paul's letter to the Romans when he speaks about praying for our government has nothing to do with our position in Christ. So do not use that to validate praying for political persons as solutions for this world. People who do that are not acquainted with their true origin nor have they met the resurrected Christ.

Do I think God will use all things and people to get our attention? Absolutely, but this world and its system is not God's priority, and neither should it be yours. We are led by His Spirit and Headship not a political party or government.

B. THE LIE THAT PERPETUATES MEDICINE

If you believe God created man to steward the earth, then it is impossible to believe the planet could produce a virus that would destroy God's creation. Yet thousands upon thousands who believe God is all powerful are desperately waiting on a vaccine to save them.

Over and over, we have made the point that nothing from the outside or the external environment is more powerful than what Christ placed in your spirit upon resurrection.

Nevertheless, the more information you have the better equipped you become in the battle to stay ever present and conscious of His resurrection.

The fundamental belief in the earth today about germs and viruses began from the false interpretations of Louis Pasteur study, which declared they are lethal, and we are helpless victims.

Now let me expose you to a different approach. Ethel Douglas Hume wrote in her book, *"Béchamp or Pasteur? A Lost Chapter in the History of Biology"*:

> *"The modern paradigm of medicine is mostly based on the germ theory of microbes invading our bodies and causing disease, allegedly a process that creates the need for a war against microbes to eliminate them all and conquer all diseases. Fear is the motivation for creating the weapons of antibiotics, antivirals and vaccines befitting this concept, but our modern population is sicker than ever.*

Are the weapons creating chronic debilitating diseases in exchange for acute illnesses considered infectious that most manage to get over with a renewed resilience to the dreaded pathogenic microbes blamed for all illness? Are we actually destroying our immune systems with our war on microbes?

Ever since Pasteur's claim to fame as the father of the germ theory, our overall health has decreased even while lifespans have increased. But during Pasteur's late 19th century – early 20th century media dominance and since then till now, there have been many scientists denouncing Pasteur's model of disease, even providing evidence that he was a plagiarist and fraud[4]."

Pasteur convinced the medical community that all germs were formed by the "magic" of spontaneous generation. He believed living matter could spontaneously be created from nonliving matter.

He later modified his belief because of the work by a German scientist named Béchamp whose experiments in fermentation proved that death and disease are not the result of outside germs invading a healthy host.

He went on to prove all organic material decomposes and joins other organic matter in the "dying" stages.

In other words, human beings whose immune system is compromised and unhealthy are attracting decomposition.

4 Béchamp or Pasteur? A Lost Chapter in the History of Biology", by Ethel Douglas Hume, first published in 1923

The remedy is proper nutrition and lack of stress, not vaccinations or medications as the medical and pharmaceutical industry would like you to believe.

The Encyclopedia Britannica says in the entry on bacteriology:

> *"The common idea of bacteria in the minds of most people is that of a hidden and sinister scourge lying in wait for mankind. This popular conception is born of the fact that attention was first focused upon bacteria through the discovery, some 70 years ago, of the relationship of bacteria to disease in man, and that in its infancy the study of bacteriology was a branch of medical science. Relatively few people assign to bacteria the important position in the world of living things that they rightly occupy, for it is only a few of the bacteria known today that have developed in such a way that they can live in the human body, and for every one of this kind, there are scores of others which are perfectly harmless and far from being regarded as the enemies of mankind, must be numbered among his best friends.*
>
> *It is in fact no exaggeration to say that upon the activities of bacteria the very existence of man depends; indeed, without bacteria there could be no other living thing in the world; for every animal and plant owes its existence to the fertility of the soil and this in turn depends upon the activity of the micro-organisms which inhabit the soil in almost inconceivable numbers."*

Therefore, bacteria found in man and animals do not cause disease but rather form a much greater purpose than the world has been led to believe.

They have the same function as those found in the soil, or in sewage, or elsewhere in nature; they are there to rebuild dead or diseased tissues, or rework body wastes, and it is well known that they will not or cannot attack healthy tissues.

Moreover, without bacteria and fungi our planet would be over its head in dead organic matter including human carcasses.

The adoption of Pasteur's erroneous theories and doctrine concerning germs or bacteria strengthened sciences hold over the populations and fostered the belief that man is a victim of his environment.

Furthermore, the germ phobia he created led to countries adopting pasteurization, which is responsible for eliminating bacteria our bodies need to reproduce healthy organs and cells.

His theory is one of the early lies in the modern-day tower of Babel. This edifice that exalts man as god is built on the foundation of science, which believes all life is an accident of evolution.

Pride will not allow man to admit that a greater being than himself both created and sustains man. God requires faith for communication and trust. Man would rather believe his senses and instruments that always validate his belief because they are formed inside this dimension.

The beginning of this decade will be remembered for

many "firsts" but, perhaps, nothing more meaningful than the realization that the modern day "Church" messages are helpless against the fear of death. The reason is they do not believe Christ destroyed death at resurrection, even if they preach it.

After you know that Jesus returned the invisible kingdom of God to this planet your attention will immediately shift its focus from the material to the spiritual. No one's life will ever change in this world until they experience the resurrected Christ.

God has always overseen and protected His creations, and nothing will ever change that because of what He did through Jesus. That reality must be front and center in the way we perceive our physical environment.

He is inside each of us with the ever-present reminder that He is uniting His creation to Himself in the present moment. If your mind wanders from that position, stop, and reconnect. Don't condemn yourself!

Over time the latency period between losing consciousness and staying present will shrink and what's more important your fascination with this realm will disappear.

CONCLUSION

YOU ALREADY KNEW BUT
NOW YOU BELIEVE

We have arrived at the part of the book where I want to reiterate some things that will provide you with the keys to changing both your physical and spiritual condition. This is not the end of the book but rather the end of a diving board.

It will be up to you to dive into the depths of His mercy and grace.

You already know that you are more spirit than flesh, which means the physical world is not your source. This is the war Jesus won, but each day we must fight the program inside our mind that tells us otherwise.

Our spiritual design for communication is one heart and mind, whose signal is faith. Our Father is both sending and receiving that wavelength to all those In Him before the foundation of the world.

The major key for that battle is remaining conscious of each moment and thought as it passes before us like the wind in a storm. The more we stay conscious the larger electromagnetic field we construct around our physical bodies that will attract the love of God.

How we think and how we feel produce the electromagnetic field around our physical bodies.

When we exhibit emotions of love, thanksgiving and joy the magnetic field around our bodies can expand to nine meters in circumference. This is significant because we are broadcasting and receiving frequencies outside time and space.

When we are both feeling and thinking love, the energy we receive from God will be greater than the signal we send. Why?

Remember, the picture of Oneness in nature called "emergence"? The Head is Christ, and He is speaking to His creation. He is sending wholeness in the form of love but unless our thoughts and feelings are one, we are unable to receive that frequency.

Most people desire happiness and freedom but are living with resentment, bitterness, anger, rejection, hostility, unforgiveness and lack. That is a mind and heart in opposition and separation, which will not receive His love.

Our preoccupation with personal identity is born from feelings of separation, which occurs when our attention leaves the present moment to focus on our external environment.

Perhaps, you still feel helpless to change your condition. Here are things to do right away to change.

First, stop believing the lie that we are victims of our surroundings and must depend on the outer world for our resources. This is one of the messages that is programmed into your subconscious at birth along with the belief that to prosper or be happy one must depend on their senses.

The only physical event that occurred in our external world that changed mankind's history for life was the resurrection of Christ. PERIOD!

All other events from that point till now or in the future is God's wake up call to those in Him before the foundation of the world.

Secondly, and the most important is that you cannot fear death because that is the belief that makes the human race selfish and frightened. In other words, as long as one believes they are mortal they will stand at the foot of the cross waiting on Jesus to return.

The fear of death produces stress that elevates anxiety to levels that destroy organs and cells because all our attention is on our body, environment, and time. Moreover, stress is the number one reason people seek physicians for physical problems, which you can change by paying attention to now.

Jesus provided everything we could ever need at His resurrection and called it His Kingdom. In fact, He said it was the most important thing in life for prosperity and peace.

> *Do not be over-anxious, therefore, asking 'What shall we eat?' or 'What shall we drink?' or 'What shall we wear?' For all these are questions that Gentiles are always asking.*
>
> *but your Heavenly Father knows that you need these things—all of them.* ***But make His Kingdom and righteousness your chief aim, and then these things shall all be given you in addition.***
>
> **Matthew 6:31-33 WEY**

Our unconscious programming, which is running 90% of the time is mostly negative. That program has made us self-fulfilling prophets of our failures. So how do you stop the self-sabotage? The most effective way to stop the unconscious program is to observe your thoughts.

When you are not separated by thoughts of what you do not have, the Holy Spirit will remind you of what He gave us. This is so important for you to grasp.

When you remain in the present moment your body will experience wholeness because you feel gratitude and thanksgiving by doing so, your body will be flooded with hormones of oxytocin, dopamine, serotonin, and endorphins that will reinforce the bodies wholeness and health. The feelings of worry and stress vanish.

The best way to perform this is to focus on breathing. Notice that your mind wanders in relationship with your breathing. Persons who breathe fast or irregularly do so as they move from thought to thought.

After you become aware of this, observe your thoughts and breathe deeply. Continue this process until you feel the peace that passes understanding bathe your body and brain. Now, continue observing your thoughts and refuse to leave that moment.

Unbelief creates mayhem, which leads to disorder and our inability to concentrate. You may think you are a believer but if your attention is on material more than spirit it is because you are still frightened. The material dimension is in chaos because man is not in harmony with God. You cannot change how you think until you "see" God's kingdom.

The picture should be crystal clear to you by now. We are more spirit than material, but our subconscious programming and fear have frightened us into believing otherwise. Now you know better. What will you do?

We are living in the most exciting times of any generation because the choice is so clear. Believe the lies from this world or fight to consciously experience God in the eternal present moment.

God provides us His eternal love each moment but unless we take time to observe and celebrate that gift, we will be waiting on something external to change our spiritual condition.

Perhaps, the most important thing you can do is begin thanking God for each incredible moment. There will never be another one more precious than the one you experience in that second.

They are pieces of eternity wrapped as a gift to you. Can you feel how extraordinary that gift is? There is no guarantee of another one. That is why each second must be celebrated by your attention. When you see this as more precious than all the gold or silver on the planet your life has changed!

The resurrection generation is not a future race of people that will inherit the earth. We are that generation each time we enter His eternal present moment that was manifested on the day He destroyed death.

Resurrection is the victory and authority over the death that has formed and controls this world.

Christ is the only inoculation you will ever need. It is the vaccination the world needs to change the way they think.

I told you from the beginning that you knew what is being written here before the foundation of the world but now you remember.

Awake!

Life Begins!

THE
RESURRECTION
GENERATION

Get this book and more in
eBook digital format

The Resurrection Generation

The Last Adam

Who Has Bewitched You?

Before the Foundation
of the World

Available on Amazon, iTunes, and our online store

www.voiceofthelight.com

If you enjoyed this book, we also recommend

Before the Foundation of the World

This jaw-dropping revelation will reacquaint you with the wisdom and riches that were implanted in your spirit before you were flesh and blood. This book will be the tool God uses to awaken your spirit to the reality of your view next to Christ, in the Heavenly places.

The key to the book of Revelation and all Biblical prophecy is inside the revelation of *The Christ*. Those with the courage to make the journey will discover that the only one keeping you from the mysteries of God's hidden truths is you. This book will be one of the most important reads for the next several generations. Do not pass up your divine intervention with the reality of what you witnessed *before the foundation of the world*.

Available on Amazon and our online store

www.voiceofthelight.com

If you enjoyed this book, we also recommend

The Last Adam

Get ready because the veil that has hidden your true nature and identity is about to be ripped off of you forever! And the gospel preached by the last Adam is the power for your transformation. This isn't a how-to book to improve your current status. It's the key that will unlock what you already knew before the foundation of the world. Do you want to reclaim what Adam lost?

Man was created in the image of the One who created all things. The last Adam was not only resurrected over death, but He also defeated the fear of it. If you've ever been afraid it's because you haven't been told the truth about your true identity. Today, when you hear His voice, take that first step into overcoming fear forever. That's what the last Adam gave us. Now, the choice is yours - but you need to take it!

Available on Amazon and our online store

www.voiceofthelight.com

If you enjoyed this book, we also recommend

Who Has Bewitched You?

There is nothing more important than the crucifixion and resurrection of Jesus Christ. It is what defines the superiority of Christianity over every other religion in the world. This book will expose you to the greatest witchcraft ever perpetuated in the Church, which is the mixing of truth with lies. There is no doubt Jesus was resurrected, but to twist the fact that He was in the earth 3 days and 3 nights, by celebrating Good Friday and Easter Sunday, takes away the accuracy and power of every prophetic scripture written about Him as our Messiah. When one's conscience compromises to adapt the Truth to tradition, we also break the shield against deception. This is not just any book, it is the most powerful weapon you will ever need to unlock the prophetic in the Bible, to dismantle any lie and to live by His Truth. You will have the key to the mysteries of God hidden for generations.

Available on Amazon and our online store

www.voiceofthelight.com

Participate in our video course series

www.voiceofthelight.com

Watch us on **Frequencies of Glory TV** and **YouTube**
Follow us on **Facebook**, **Instagram** and **Twitter**

www.frequenciesofglorytv.com
www.youtube.com/user/VoiceoftheLight

https://m.facebook.com/AnaMendezFerrellPaginaOficial
www.instagram.com/emerson.ferrell
www.twitter.com/MendezFerrell

Contact us today!

Voice of The Light Ministries
P.O. Box 3418
Ponte Vedra, FL. 32004
USA
904-834-2447

www.voiceofthelight.com